Light and Consciousness: Soul Food for the Starving Mind

Volume 2

Brandon Zackery

History has its eyes on you

Copyright 2023 Brandon Zackery

All Rights Reserved

ISBN: 9798854598903

History has its eyes on you

Dedication

This set is dedicated to the Black and Brown educators of the world who are forced to stick to a pre-set curriculum irrelevant to the development of the Black and Brown students under your care. We know you are trying to teach Black and Brown kids information vital to their stratification while also trying to stay employed within the system of white supremacy.

———This volume is dedicated to my children, Ayanna Nicole Blair and Alexander King Zackery. You are forced to evolve in a time when education is weaponized, and history is systematically erased. I'm doing my part to intervene and combat the racist system that now permeates your existence. I hope it is enough and you are inspired to continue the fight.

The concept of equal education should be abandoned in favor of a philosophy and approach appropriate to one's needs. The function of education and intelligence is to solve problems particular to a people and nation and to secure that people's and that nation's biological survival. Any philosophy of education or approach which failed to do so is inadequate." -Dr. Amos Wilson

Table of Contents

Authors Note: 13

Introduction: 15

Chapter 1: The White-Looking Black People of East Jackson, Ohio: **21**

Chapter 2: The Outlawing of Mary Jane and Its Racist Past: **25**

Chapter 3: Twerking: The Origins of Worshiping Through Dance: **28**

Chapter 4: The Lynching of Benjamin Hart: **31**

Chapter 5: The Ghost of Henrietta Marie: **33**

Chapter 6: Benjamin Lay: The Dwarf Who Stood Tall Against Racism: **36**

Chapter 7: The Exorcism of Latoya Ammons: When the Devil Came for a Black Family: **39**

Chapter 8: C.O. Chinn: The Baddest S.O.B. in Mississippi: **43**

Chapter 9: The Bad-Ass Librarians of Timbuktu: **47**

Chapter 10: Thomas Downing: The Oyster King of New York: **50**

Chapter 11: Molly Williams: The First Black Female Firefighter: **53**

Chapter 12: The Power of "X." How Black People Used Their Signature to Fight Racism: **56**

Chapter 13: Robert Johnson: The Man Who Sold His Soul to The Devil: **58**

Chapter 14: Outlawing Dunking: How Racism Stained the Game of Basketball: **61**

Chapter 15: The Defenders: A Secret Militant Organization of Tuscaloosa, Alabama: **64**

Chapter 16: Pearls: A Story of Slavery, Women of Color, and Trade: **67**

Chapter 17: The Groveland Four: When White Women Lie: **70**

Chapter 18: African American Black Heritage and the Juneteenth Flag: **74**

Chapter 19: Cat-Hauling: A Cruel and Unusual Punishment: **77**

Chapter 20: The Kissing Case of 1958: Childs Play and the Consequences of White Lies: **80**

Chapter 21: Major Taylor: The Man Who Searched for a Rival and Never Found One: **83**

Chapter 22: Queen Charlotte of Mecklenburg: The Black Royal: **87**

Chapter 23: Tippu Tip: The Most Prolific Slave Trader of All-Time: **90**

Chapter 24: The Kushites and The Black Pharaoh Who Brought Egypt to Her Knees: **93**

Chapter 25: The Greatest Clarinet Player Ever. That's It. That's the Whole Title: **98**

Chapter 26: Brothers in and Out of Bondage. An Examination of Free Blacks Who Enslaved People: **101**

Chapter 27: Mac and Cheese: How an American Classic Had its Roots in Blackness: **105**

Chapter 28: Integrating the Sky: The First Black Paratrooper of the US Military: **109**

Chapter 29: What Could Have Been: America's First HBCU That Didn't Happen: **112**

Chapter 30: Do You Have the Password: Black Secret Societies and Clandestine Organizations in the Negro Community: **116**

Chapter 31: Black Smoke: A History of African American BBQ Traditions: **121**

Chapter 32: Discovering King Tut's Tomb: Give Credit Where Credit Is Due: **127**

Chapter 33: Climbing to God: The All-Black Group That Scaled Mount Everest: **130**

Chapter 34: The Wereth Eleven: The Forgotten Black Soldiers of WWII: **133**

Chapter 35: Black Women and Violence: A Gendered Analysis of Armed Resistance: **137**

Chapter 36: The Case of Willie Francis, the Black Teen Who Got the Electric Chair Twice: **141**

Chapter 37: The History of the Highway System: **144**

Chapter 38: Identifying Unknown Graves of the Enslaved: **147**

Chapter 39: Black Pirates: Men of African Descent on the High Seas: **150**

Chapter 40: Pablo Picasso: Plagiarism and Denial: **153**

Check on Learning

1. What is so significant about the Black residents in East Jackson, Ohio?
2. Why was marijuana outlawed in America?
3. What is the name of today's popular dance that originates in African spirituality and worship?
4. This young, Black man was lynched for being accused of looking through a window.
5. The "ghost" of Henrietta Marie is a famous seafaring relic from antebellum.
6. What is the name of the dwarf who stood up to racism?
7. This Black woman and her family lived in a haunted house and battled demons.
8. This man from Mississippi stood up to racism until he was labeled a "crazy negro" by the townspeople.
9. Who were the people who smuggled the books out of Timbuktu ahead of an invasion by Al Qaida militants?
10. This Black man became known as "The Oyster King of New York."

11. This Black woman is remembered as the first Black firefighter.

12. What letter did illiterate enslaved people use to sign their names?

13. This blues player is said to have met the devil at the crossroads and sold his soul.

14. The NCAA and the NBA outlawed this basketball move because Blacks used it to dominate the game.

15. This clandestine group of men in Tuscaloosa, Alabama, defended the Black residents with violence against Klan aggression.

16. This symbolic jewel comes from the depths of the sea and is adorned by Black women all over.

17. In Groveland, Florida, four young Black men were falsely accused of raping a white woman. They became known as what?

18. These two flags are prominent in Black culture and represent heritage and emancipation.

19. What is the name of the cruel and unusual punishment utilized by enslavers involving a cat?

20. Two Black children spent months imprisoned after a white child claimed to do this innocent act with them.

21. He was the victim of racism, yet he was still considered the fastest cyclist in the world during his time.

22. This Black queen of Mecklenburg has a city in North Carolina named after her.

23. This African man was considered the most prolific slave trader of all time.

24. The ancient Egyptians sought to erase this 25th dynasty from history.

25. This Black woman musical prodigy still plays her clarinet on the streets of the French Quarters in New Orleans.

26. Sometimes enslaved Black people in America were owned by these unlikely enslavers.

27. This dish of Italian origin and various cheeses is essential to Black food culture.

28. This Black man was the first to put his "feet and knees together in the wind" and earn these particular wings in the US military.

29. This particular type of school for a marginalized group was set to be the first of its kind in 1831 in Connecticut.
30. These organization types used secrecy, passwords, and handshakes to identify members.
31. This term refers to an elderly enslaved man who was an expert cook and led the effort to prepare smoked meat for the slaveholders.
32. This young Egyptian boy discovered the tomb of another young Egyptian boy, leading to the most famous archeological find in modern history.
33. The all-Black climbing group known as Full Circle climbed to the summit of this famous mountain in 2022.
34. These eleven Black men fought against Nazi Germany and were forgotten by the US government.
35. Black women used this resistance method, generally only associated with men, to fight back against racial violence.
36. What is the name of the Black teenager who was falsely convicted, imprisoned, and given the electric chair twice?
37. The Dwight D. Eisenhower Highway system was built for this specific reason.

38. What is the name of the final resting place of enslaved people that is sometimes marked with seashells, yucca plants, and pink quartz?

39. What is the name of this Black pirate that served alongside Black Beard on Queen Anne's Revenge?

40. This famous painter of cubism plagiarized African art without ever acknowledging its influence.

Author's Note

The idea for this monograph was born out of the social media era, which showed us the capacity, volume, and speed by which an influencer can spread information. After using popular social media platforms to spread vital history, I committed to putting that information into a book. I understand people are not a monolith and do not ingest information similarly. As an avid reader, I wanted to create a book, especially for those who still enjoy the feel of turning pages and digesting black words against white paper. Therefore, I present a body of work born online but now available between monograph covers.

As an author, historian, advocate, and educator, I am invested in the stratification of my people and those who ally with the revolutionary struggle.

I am well into adulthood and only now fully understand how much information was hidden from us. The research that went into uncovering these short, 3-minute introductions helped to appease my appetite to learn more. I hope that it does the same for others. I don't see any information about Africans in the diaspora as particularly more valuable than others. But I am genuinely concerned about the amount of data we aren't unaware of. I've discovered that many stories of triumph, success, and perseverance have never been revealed. I aim to become a great excavator and show what has been in the shadows for so long.

Information is currency, and I am trying to make everyone within reach wealthy. History has its eyes on you and me.

Introduction

I found myself in a debate with another regarding a very poignant question that was posed. We were asked, "What is the most important subject for a developing Black youth?" I listened to my debate opponent argue their perspective regarding mathematics. Their official answer was economics, but they understood that economics is not typically a class offered to Black youth in the public school system. They leveraged their argument on the belief that the problems. Black people today face the result of misinformation and a lack of understanding around money. I listened with open ears as he glided through his perspective regarding finances. I agreed with much of his analysis, but I still wasn't convinced. In response, I offered a tailored rebuttal.

History. I believe history is the most crucial subject young Black youth can submerge themselves into. I offer this subject up in reverence because it is all-encompassing and equally foundational. If we view knowledge through the lens of architectural development, history will serve as the strong base upon which the rest of the structure is constructed. History is broad enough to support other fields of knowledge and is deeply intertwined.

History can be summed up as what one knows about themselves. What one knows about themselves will manifest into what one thinks of themselves, resulting in how one conducts themselves. History feeds directly into residual self-image. Therefore, history is critical to understanding who one is. We all can make ourselves into who we're to be. But where we come from is a legacy already written for us. The job of history is to unveil that legacy and expose the person to who they are from a historical perspective.

As a young man growing up in the era of early hip-hop, I used that genre of music as a teaching tool by which I learned about myself. Early hip-hop was instrumental in exposing young Black youth to history through rhyme and lyrics. I was particularly drawn to artists such as KRS-1 and his ability to teach me about myself through his music. I believe he accurately articulated my argument when he claimed:

> When one doesn't know about the other one's culture, Ignorance swoops down like a vulture. 'Cause Becausen't see that you aren't just a janitor, no one told you about Benjamin Banneker. A brilliant Black man that invented the almanac. Can't you see where KRS is coming from? Elie Whitney, Halie Selassi, and Grandville Woods made the walky-talky. Lewis Latimer improved on Edison. Charles Drew did a lot for medicine. Garrett Morgan made the traffic lights. Harriet Tubman freed the

enslaved people at night. Madame CJ Walker made the straightening comb, but you won't know this if you weren't shown. The point I'm getting at might be harsh because we're just walking around brainwashed.

It was lyrics of that caliber that introduced me to names, places, and events that stretched beyond the mandated Black History Month reports we had to do in grade school. I became consumed and equally fascinated by the characters of stories I wasn't exposed to within the Western education I was indoctrinated into. After having Martin Luther King Jr. shoved down my throat during my youth, learning about historical actors and actresses involved in the diasporic revolutionary struggle was refreshing. Exposure to information that had been previously denied to me became the impetus towards further study. History became my piece-de-resistance.

This monograph is about the sine qua, non-known as Enlightenment. It is constructed as an academic guide to exposing and deconstructing the global history of Africans in the diaspora. The information contained within this volume is designed and intended for readers within a wide age range to ingest, digest, and regurgitate with accuracy when needed. This monograph is my intervention in spreading knowledge among those interested in learning about and understanding the history of Black-skinned people.

The methodology employed within these pages is based on individual chapters about a specific subject. Each chapter is short, easy to understand, and designed to provide a high-level overview of a particular topic. The methodology ensures that the reader knows the topic's basics and is left with room for further research. Within these pages, the reader will be forced to grapple with various themes such as post-colonialism, religion, gender, Marxism, mythology, white supremacy, and oral traditions.

The historiography of Africans in the global diaspora is vast. Scholars have produced literary works for thousands of years regarding Africans' accomplishments, exploits, and history worldwide. My intervention in the scholarship is to compile volumes of work that introduce what I consider to be lesser-known history.

The history that is deconstructed within these volumes is history that has been purposely excluded from mainstream Western education. Many refer to this history as "hidden." It exists, yet it is not available to the masses. I aim to make this vital history available to readers seeking further enlightenment. By bringing hidden information to light, I hope to imbue the unknowing with information that will galvanize their passion and motivate them to expound upon the information presented here.

Update for Volume II

With the release of volume I, it became even more apparent how valuable this information is to the people. The response was tremendous, and I listened with enthusiasm and zeal as people exclaimed just how engaged they were in the new information they were learning. I had countless conversations with readers who discussed the information they thought they knew and how much they didn't know. I listened as people told me how important it was to learn the origins of many things they were familiar with. For instance, I dealt with origin stories such as The Black Witch of the Salem Witch Trials in Volume I. Not one reader I talked to had ever heard of Tituba and her connection to Salem. Many readers were familiar with "hamboning," as it is a staple in the Black community. Yet, none knew of its origin or its etymology. Another example is Br'er Rabbit, the trickster rabbit from Black folklore. These stories have been handed down for generations, but their origins have not been deconstructed to the average reader. That is where my monographs intervene.

I have a better understanding of my place in this space of education. Each interaction with a starving mind is a reminder of my purpose. I have renewed energy and motivation as I encounter those seeking more information. I am joyful as I watch them react to learning something new. That response to knowledge propels me to seek out, find, and present further information.

Volume II is more of that soul food readers have come to love and expect.

Chapter 1

You Don't Have to Look Black to Be Black: The White-Looking Black People of East Jackson, Ohio

Race is a construct that was created to rank people according to inherited physical and behavioral differences. Essentially, races are nothing more than cultural interventions reflecting specific attitudes and beliefs imposed on different populations in the wake of Western European conquests beginning in the 15th century. Race doesn't indeed exist. Yet, it has genuinely dire consequences. This is the story of a specific population of Black people who look white but identify as Black.

What's wrong with being Black? This question has been asked over and over in a small Ohio town. East Jackson is a poor, rural community in southern Ohio where many residents identify as Black despite appearing white. Just down the street is the much larger town of Waverly, with its lush farmland, new homes, Starbucks, restaurants, and Walmart. This contrast is a byproduct of anti-abolitionist sentiment in Waverly that began nearly 200 years ago. Ohio was established as a free state at the start of the 19th century, but those fleeing slavery in the

South by using Ohio's underground railroads avoided Waverly. It was known to be anti-abolition and anti-Black. It was also a sundown town, where Black people had to be out of town by dark or face arrest, threats, or violence.

East Jackson developed due to Blacks and anyone appearing non-white being corralled into a minor part of town. East Jackson was known as the "Black side of town," they suffered the consequences of their Blackness in the 1800s. Some were forced to live in East Jackson who were not Black, but they were treated as Black, second-class citizens. They were Black by law. The social attitude in Ohio was that one drop of "Black blood" disqualified an individual from having the legal status of whites. Over the generations, the people of East Jackson married across racial lines and had multiracial children. Because of miscegenation, Black heritage thinned out, but Black identity did not.

All the residents of East Jackson claim to be relatives. Most of them have identified as Black for most of their lives. Many older generations can run off their Black ancestors on their fingers. They also recognize how the family members married white and amalgamated white and Black into the bloodstream. What makes the residents different is a consequence of genetics. Over the generations, the residents of East Jackson have taken on the physical qualities of white people.

Today, there seems to be a paradigm shift among the younger generation. Many have severed the ties of their Black identity because they've found it easier to navigate the socio-political arenas as white. While parents struggle to maintain their Black identity, some youths have decided that their Black heritage works to prevent evolution in this race-based society. So, they now tend to identify as white. In several families, some siblings identify as Black, and others identify as White, leading to outsiders asking more and more questions.

With the introduction of technology, some residents have considered DNA tests the determining factor for their identity. At the same time, others have no intention of abandoning their Black heritage. Others struggle with the dichotomy of race and seek to pass white in public while simultaneously embracing their Black roots in private. As the older generation takes its leave from the living, so goes the residents' connection to those Blacks who traveled to Ohio in search of liberation. Perhaps the burden of identifying as Black is too much for some or not worth it to others. In this Ohio town, if you ask, "What's wrong with being Black," you will solicit a wide range of opinions from just about everyone. Now you know.

Chapter 2

The Outlawing of Mary Jane and Its Racist Past

Unfortunately, the only reason marijuana, commonly known as "Reggie," is illegal today is due to racism and xenophobia. It was purely motivated by fear and prejudice, which led to the banning of Mary Jane as a recreational drug.

The earliest colonist learned to smoke and grow the plant from the indigenous people they encountered upon arriving at these new lands. They quickly learned of its healing values and developed it for themselves. In fact, at one point, the growing of cannabis was colonial law, and every citizen with land had to produce a batch of Mary Jane. Additionally, Mary Jane could be used as currency to purchase other items or settle a debt.

Racism is directly responsible for the ban on marijuana. When Mexicans entered America, they brought Mary Jane and smoked it regularly. Many Americans' attitudes toward cannabis shifted at the turn of the century, motivated by Mexican immigration to the US. Because Mexicans like Poncho Villa and his band of outlaws refused to be controlled, their violent behavior and reaction to American imperialism were blamed on the weed they smoked. It was said that the grass gave them super strength and turned them into savages. Police officers in Texas claimed that Mary Jane incited violent crimes and aroused a "lust for blood." Mexicans brought cannabis from Mexico, and white Americans were already enjoying the effects of it going back to colonial days. Because Mexicans did not submit themselves to white rule and authority, marijuana was blamed for their "insubordination."

In 1930, Harry Anslinger became the first director of the Federal Bureau of Narcotics. Once appointed, he began a campaign based on race and violence. Anslinger did not hide his prejudice. Helped popularize "marijuana" instead of the more common name, "cannabis," to tie the drug to anti-Mexican prejudice. Between 1916 and 1931, 29 states outlawed Reggie.

Mary Jane was a prevalent recreational drug in the early music scene. Jazz and swing artists from New Orleans through the Midwest of Chicago and up into New York regularly enjoy the effects of Mary Jane. Again, it was racism that drove the racist narrative surrounding Black music artists. Jazz music was said to be "satanic" and directly result from marijuana use. The association with jazz music to weed helped push the idea that marijuana was evil.

Lastly, and probably the most disturbing fact, the 1937 marijuana ban was directly influenced by an idea circulated among the white population. That was the belief that Mary Jane made white women have a more profound desire to seek sexual relations with Black men. Because of this common belief, Mary Jane was officially banned in 1937.

Racism and xenophobia were the root cause of the outlawing of marijuana. The white demographic sought to demonize and criminalize anything tied to Mexican immigration and the Black population. Mary Jane served as the perfect conduit. Now you know.

Chapter 3

Twerking: The Origins of Worshiping Through Dance

Using the terms twerking and worship in the same sentence will solicit some vitriol looks and a cacophony of rebuttals. This is because twerking has a negative connotation today as it is intrinsically tied to being sexually provocative. Yet, a deep dive into history traces the journey of twerking from Alkebrulan to Brazil, the West Indies, and America. Furthermore, investigative research shows the relationship between what we know to be twerking today and worship in African spirituality.

Historians who have tackled the subject have identified dances identical to twerking in Charleston and New Orleans ports through the Atlantic Slave Trade. Before that, the dance could be found in the West Indies and Brazil, leading back to West Africa. The term twerking is a word combination of "twist and jerk" born out of the lexicon of New Orleans in the 1990s. Twerking as a dance has a much older history.

The origins of twerking can be traced to Côte d'Ivoire in West Africa, where a similar style of dance, known as the Mapouka dance, originated. The Mapouka dance focuses primarily on moving the buttocks with thrusting hip movements and a low squat stance, just as twerking is today. In Africa, twerking was used in various capacities, rituals, and ceremonies. For instance, the dance was used to celebrate different occasions and milestones. The birth of a child, the veneration of the ancestors, ceremonial communication, and the joining of two in union all used twerking as a part of the ceremonies. What is less known is how twerking was used in worship.

Africans have used dance, song, and chant for thousands of years to worship their deities. Through these individual displays, Africans praised their gods, asked for blessings, sought direction, and sought protection in the Orishas. Twerking did not have a sexual connotation to it. Instead, it was an acceptable display of worship. Women of various tribes and ethnic groups used the dance to enter a trance and show respect for their gods. Dance was communication. It served as a language between the devotee and the higher spiritual being.

    The legacy of colonialism devolved twerking from expression and worship to sexually based acts of provocation and seduction. Like everything else with its genesis in Africa, twerking as a spiritual expression was slowly removed from the American Black culture and replaced with a more acceptable culture rooted in proper Christian decorum. Even spiritual dances like the "ring shout" have been expelled from Black culture today.

Today, twerking has a negative aura because of society's love for misogyny, the hyper-judgment of anything not deemed Christian, and our severing from ancient African practices. Yet, twerking is a way that Black women reclaim public spaces through the motion of their bodies. Twerking is expression and artistic in nature. It is a skill that one uses to communicate with, to express joy, and to "sweat out the problems of the day," as Andre 3000 so eloquently put it.

Let us not forget that racism, Western religious influence, and patriarchal judgment condemn twerking today. Yet, its legacy going back to Alkebrulan is one of worship and reverence for the gods. Twerking is a language of its own, a forgotten language.

Chapter 4

The Lynching of Benjamin Hart: When Simply Being Accused of Looking Gets You Killed

The Goodie Mob once asked, "Who's that peeping in my window?" Some racists in Florida in 1923 said it was Benjamin Hart…and lynched him for it. White women have been responsible for many of the lynchings across America. Their lives, tears, and words were weaponized and catalyzed by horrors beyond human comprehension. This is the story of a Black man who was murdered after being falsely accused of peeping in a window.

Benjamin Hart was a farmhand in Duval County Jacksonville, Florida, in 1923. Hart was employed at a logging camp where he worked cutting timber. On 24 August, approximately ten white men came to Mr. Hart's home around 9:30 at night, claiming to be sheriff's deputies. Benjamin was surprised at their presence and frightened, for he had done nothing outside of go to work and come home as he did every day.

The nightriders accused Benjamin of peeping into the bedroom window of a young white girl. The girl was not there to identify Benjamin, nor did she have a description of the alleged perpetrator. The white men also picked up four Black men sleeping in a cabin near the logging camp. Hart professed his innocence and denied such conduct, but the men detained him and said they were taking him to the country jail. Benjamin Hart never made it.

Gunshots woke the few people living near Kings Road and 12th Street, who reported seeing six cars of white men leaving the area. Shortly after midnight the next day, Ben Hart's handcuffed and bullet-riddled body was found in a ditch about three miles from the city. He had been shot six times at close range. Police investigating Ben Hart's murder soon determined he was at his home some 12 miles away when the alleged peeping incident occurred. Sheriff W.H. Dowling was quoted in the newspaper the next day as saying, "They lynched an innocent negro." He promised those responsible would be arrested, but no charges were ever filed.

Benjamin Hart was terrorized, bound, beaten, and murdered because of a lie. He was not a peeping tom. Instead, he was a Black man whose life was cut short because of the insatiable lust for Black blood that racist whites in the old South harbored. Now you know.

Chapter 5

The Ghost of Henrietta Marie: When the Ocean Gives Up Its Dead

Henrietta Marie was no woman. Instead, she was a ship, a slave ship that carried Africans in bondage to a new world and away from Alkebrulan. She is one of the essential slave ships not because of what she represents but rather because of the ghost she yielded to the world today.

There is no denying the fact that the Trans-Atlantic slave trade took place. The evidence is irrefutable. Yet, maritime physical evidence has been lacking due to a significant number of reasons. When slavery was outlawed, slavers would scuttle their boats not to be caught. The punishment for slavery was to be put to death in many cases. To avoid that, many slave ships were intentionally destroyed to avoid detection. The recently discovered *Cotilda* in Alabama is an example. Lousy weather took many boats to the ocean bottom, as did piracy and sabotage.

Henrietta Marie is just another piece of physical evidence that deconstructs the ignorance of those who suggest the Trans-Atlantic slave trade didn't happen. Holocaust deniers always point to a lack of physical evidence, and Henrietta refutes that claim.

The seas are unforgiving, and very few ships have survived well enough to be studied. The *Henrietta Marie* is an exception. She was constructed in France in the 17th century. She fell into English hands and was repurposed for the slave trade. She made at least two voyages from Africa to the West Indies. On her first voyage in 1697, she carried over 200 African captives to Barbados as chattel property.

Records show that in 1699, *Henrietta* left England to secure Africans and trade goods in Guinea Coast and on to Port Royal, Jamaica. She attempted to avoid the pirate waters between Cuba and Hispaniola to sail back to England safely. She wrecked in the reef about 35 miles west of Key West, Florida. There were no survivors, and *Henrietta Marie* lay silent on the ocean bottom for almost three hundred years.

The first to find *Henrietta* was a treasure-hunting team in 1972. When they realized they had discovered a slave ship and not a treasure ship, they reburied the artifacts, covered the ship's hull, and left the site without a word. In 1983, Henry Taylor rediscovered the wreck of the *Henrietta Marie.*

What makes the ghost of *Henriette Marie* so fascinating and historically significant is that Henrietta Marie has yielded more than 7000 objects, the most extensive collection of artifacts from any slave ship. Eighty shackles, leg, and neck irons were also discovered at the site, along with other artifacts organic to the vessel.

In May 1993, the National Association of Black Scuba Divers placed a memorial plaque on the site of *Henrietta Marie*. The plaque faces the African shore thousands of miles away and has the name of the slave ship, and reads, "In memory and recognition of the courage, pain, and suffering of enslaved African people. Speak her name and gently touch the souls of our ancestors."

The *Henrietta Marie* was no woman. Instead, she is a ghost of a painful past that reminds us of the horrors of bondage connecting our ancestral world to the New World. Now you know.

Chapter 6

Benjamin Lay: The Dwarf Who Stood Tall Against Slavery

Benjamin Lay was born in 1682; his parents were Quakers who migrated from England. After a quick stay in London and a marriage in 1718, Lay moved to Barbados as a merchant. Here, he began advocating for the abolition of slavery after he witnessed an enslaved man commit suicide rather than be whipped again by his owner.

In 1731, Lay emigrated to Philadelphia and settled into a Quaker colony. It was here that his reputation took root. Benjamin Lay was only 4 feet tall and slightly hunchback. His chest protruded oddly, and his arms were as long as his legs. He was a vegetarian; he ate only fruits, vegetables, and honey and drank only milk and water. He did not believe humans were superior to non-human animals and created his clothes to boycott the slave-labor industry. He would not wear or eat anything made from the loss of animal life or provided by any degree of slave labor. Refusing to participate in what he described in his writings as a degraded, hypocritical, tyrannical, and even demonic society, Lay was committed to a lifestyle of almost complete self-sustenance after his beloved wife died. He was known to the town folks as "Little Benjamin."

He was an outspoken opponent of slavery long before most Quakers did. Lay was notorious for using force to draw attention to slavery. He once stood barefoot and, in the snow, outside a Quaker meeting in the dead of winter. When a passerby expressed concern about his health, he said enslaved people were forced to work outside in the winter dressed as he was. On another occasion, he kidnapped a slaveholder's infant to demonstrate how Africans felt when their relatives were sold overseas.

The most noteworthy act occurred in 1738 at the Philadelphia Yearly Meeting of Quakers in Burlington, New Jersey. He closed a diatribe against slavery, dressed as a soldier, by referencing the Bible and stating that all men should be equal under God. He thrust a sword into a Bible carrying a bladder of blood-red pokeberry juice, which spattered all over.

Benjamin Lay lived in the Pennsylvania countryside in a cave with outside access. He raised goats and fruit trees and wove his flax into garments. He kept his library inside the cave: 200 books on theology, biography, history, and poetry. He was remembered for his generosity rather than his peculiarities. He wrote almost 200 pamphlets, most of which were passionate polemics against different social institutions of the day, notably slavery, the capital penalty, and the Quaker elite.

Benjamin Franklin and Lay were great friends. Franklin printed Lay's tirade against slavery, *All Slave Keepers That Keep the Innocent in Bondage, Apostates*, and sold a copy for two shillings. Franklin then enslaved a man called Joseph, and by 1750, he had two more enslaved people, Peter and Jemima. Lay prodded him for an explanation: "*With What Right?*" Franklin drafted a second will in April 1757, guaranteeing Peter and Jemima would be liberated after his death.

Benjamin Lay died in Abington, Pennsylvania, in 1759. Benjamin Lay was buried in Abington in a grave whose exact location is unknown. In 2018, the Pennsylvania Historical and Museum Commission erected a historical marker in Abington commemorating Lay. Now you know.

Chapter 7

The Exorcism of Latoya Ammons: When the Devil Came for a Black Family

Often when we hear about exorcisms, we expect to hear about non-Black people such as Emily Rose, Roland Doe (from which the movie The Exorcist was based), and Anneliese Michel. Hollywood and mainstream media have yet to grapple with exorcism and the Black community. Some predominantly Black churches have claimed to have performed exorcisms during revivals going back to antebellum times. Yet, exorcisms and Black people have a divide between them that makes them seem more far-fetched than mainstream. Yet at least one documented exorcism on a Black family involved a group of credible, non-Black witnesses. This is the exorcism of Latoya Ammons.

In 2011, a woman and her three children claimed to be haunted and possessed by demonic forces. They moved into a house on Carolina Street in Gary, Indiana. Almost immediately upon moving in, big black flies began swarming their screened-in porch, even though it was winter in Indiana.

Ammons testified that after midnight, she occasionally heard the steady clump of footsteps climbing the basement stairs and the creak of the door opening between the basement and kitchen. No one was there. Even after they locked the door, the noise continued. Campbell said she awoke one night and saw a shadowy figure of a man pacing her living room. She leaped out of bed to investigate and found large, wet boot prints.

One night about 2 AM, Latoya heard the screams of children, and she ran into their bedroom to find her 12-year-old granddaughter levitating above the bed unconscious. The girl fell back into the bed and woke up without remembering what happened. Several adults and children witnessed this.

Latoya Ammons called some local churches, but most refused to listen. Officials at one church told them the Carolina Street House had spirits in it. They recommended that the family clean the home with bleach and ammonia, then use oil to draw crosses on every door and window. Campbell and Ammons also told *The Star* they reached out to two clairvoyants, who said more than 200 demons besieged the family's home.

The family said demons possessed Ammons and her children, then ages 7, 9, and 12. The kids' eyes bulged, evil smiles crossed their faces, and their voices deepened every time it happened. The youngest boy, then 7, sat in a closet talking to a boy that no one else could see. The other boy was describing what it felt like to be killed.

Finally, in desperation, they went to their family physician, Dr. Geoffrey Onyeukwu, on April 19, 2012. Ammons' sons cursed Onyeukwu in demonic voices, raging at him. Medical staff said the youngest boy was "lifted and thrown into the wall with nobody touching him," according to a DCS report. Someone from the doctor's office called 911. Onyeukwu said seven or eight police officers and multiple ambulances showed up.

Meanwhile, someone called the Department of Children Services (DCS) and asked the agency to investigate Ammons for possible child abuse or neglect. While a caretaker from DCS was interviewing the 7-year-old boy, he started growling, and his eyes rolled back in his head. According to the original DCS report - an account corroborated by the nurse and agent from DCS, the 9-year-old walked backward up the wall to the ceiling, flipped over, landed back on the ground, and stood staring at them.

Eventually, a local priest from St. Stephen Parish got permission from the Catholic church to perform an exorcism. The Gary Police chief and several other officers witnessed the hauntings and possessions—several church officials, the family of the Ammons, and DCS case workers. Netflix picked up the story of Latoya Ammons and her kids. Now you know.

Chapter 8

C.O. Chinn: The Baddest S.O.B. in Mississippi

The civil rights movement has been historized as a nonviolent movement. Pacifists and proponents of moral suasion have driven this narrative to closely align themselves with the teachings of Dr. King and Gandhi, among others. What historians have reckoned with in the last several decades is that nothing could be further from the truth. The civil rights movement was violent, and many gains during that time were made possible through violence or the threat of violence. Sometimes even pacifists stuck to a nonviolent philosophy and had to outsource violence to get their agenda across. This is the story of C.O. Chinn, the Black man who shook up Madison County, Mississippi.

You won't ever read about him in your history books, which is a purposeful omission. Chinn's exploits shook the foundations of a so-called non-violent movement, and his exploits (and the actions of many others) caused a paradigm shift in history.

Chinn was born on 18 September 1919 to a family that owned 154 acres in Farmhaven, Madison County. Later in life, he held a cafe on Franklin Street, and his wife and children were active in civil rights work. The Chinn family frequently provided shelter and protection for civil rights workers who came into town in Mississippi. The Chinn's property was said to be the "safest place in all of Mississippi" because of the number of guns and C.O. Chinn's willingness to use them to protect his guest. He ran a thriving bootlegging business and owned a juke joint where James Brown performed.

Chinn earned a reputation early in life as completely fearless of white folks. He was tall, dark, and muscular. Chinn's folks were independent farmers his entire life, and they had a strict rule, "never work for white folks." One day, a white farmer approached his mother and told her that Chinn needed to find work with a white person or leave the county. When she told her son about it, Chinn went to the farmer, shoved a .38 pistol between his eyes, and told him to stay out of Chinn's family affairs. Chinn was known around town as that "crazy negro," and because whites fashioned him as crazy, they labeled him "dangerous."

Although Chinn labored in the civil rights movement, he did not subscribe to being non-violent. Mamie Chinn once said, "My husband has never been a nonviolent man. He'd fight the devil out of Hell if he had to." In 1963 in Canton, Mississippi, Chinn attended a bond hearing for a Student Non-Violent Coordinating Committee (SNCC) volunteer arrested on a trumped-up traffic violation. Chinn walked into the courtroom with a holstered pistol visible on his hip. The judge yelled at C.O. that he couldn't come in here wearing that gun. Madison County sheriff and hardline racist Billy Noble was also in the courtroom. Chinn looked at Noble and said, "As long as that son of a b*tch over there is wearing his gun, I'm going to wear mine." People in the courtroom expected a shootout right on the spot. Noble didn't want any smoke and backed down. After the incident, Sheriff Noble said, "There are only two bad sons of bitches in the county, me and that n*gger C.O. Chinn."

Whites in Madison County flat-out feared Chinn. Members of SNCC and the Congress for Racial Equality (CORE) outsourced violence to C.O. Chinn. Because these organizations subscribed to a nonviolent philosophy, they allowed Chinn to handle anything for them that required violence. C.O. had no qualms about using violence to defend his people. He often sat outside the church with a shotgun in full view, daring someone to act like they were there to harm.

Even violently, Chinn's commitment to protecting his people did have consequences. He lost his businesses and his property. He was more about action than talk and was accused of shooting a man in the arm who attempted to bomb the Mississippi Freedom Democratic Party headquarters. He was found guilty of the charges, but the Mississippi Supreme Court reversed the decision based on the prosecution's prejudicial instructions and substantial errors. 1970 Chinn was found guilty of killing another man, Vernon Ricks. He claimed it was in self-defense but was found guilty. He served almost a decade in prison before being released.

    He returned to his civil rights work, and before his death on 19 July 1999 from colon cancer, Chinn saw his son, Robert, and daughter-in-law, Mamie Chinn, become judges. Now you know.

Chapter 9

The Bad-Ass Librarians of Timbuktu: The True Story of the Race to Save The World's Most Precious Manuscripts.

Timbuktu is a city in Mali, just north of the Niger River. By 1325, the great Mansa Musa visited the town, and it became a center for the trade of gold, salt, ivory, and enslaved peoples. In addition to those commodities, it was a center of the manuscript trade, with traders bringing Islamic texts from all over the Muslim world. At its height, Timbuktu boasted several prestigious universities and was considered the scholarly center of Africa. To the people of Timbuktu, literacy and books were symbols of wealth, power, and blessings, and the acquisition of books became a primary concern for scholars.

In 2012, the city came under attack from militant hardline Islamists who didn't hold the sacred text as part of their Islamic heritage. Rather, they viewed it as idolatry that contradicted their interpretation of Islam, backed by al-Qaida, the militant Islamists set about destroying critical cultural icons in the city. Librarians feared that the sacred text of Timbuktu would be followed.

Librarian Abdel Kader Haidara organized and oversaw a secret plot to smuggle 350,000 medieval manuscripts out of Timbuktu. Abdel Kader Haidara was a son of a scholar and an explorer, and he grew up in an intellectual environment in Timbuktu. He often traveled across the Sahara on camelback and up the rivers exploring smaller villages. In 1984, the head of the Ahmed Baba Institute, the government-owned library in Timbuktu, called on Haidara to travel around northern Mali, tracking down these manuscripts that had been lost, buried, and disappeared over generations. Reluctant at first, Haidara accepted the responsibility, and for the next 12 years, he traveled around Mali collecting scholarly manuscripts.

On Friday morning, 25 January 2013, fifteen jihadis entered the restoration and conservation rooms on the ground floor of the Ahmed Baba Institute in Sankoré. The militants swept 4,202 manuscripts off lab tables and shelves and carried them into the tiled courtyard. They doused the manuscripts in gasoline and set the ancient text on fire.

Many of the city's manuscripts were hidden in cellars, buried in the sand, between the mosque's mud walls, and safeguarded by their patrons. This is how many of these manuscripts survived the city's decline and previous invasions. The librarians of Timbuktu knew the importance of this ancient text and took steps to safeguard them for generations.

How the librarians were able to outsmart the militants of al-Qaida is something out of *Ocean's 13* movies. The librarians went to great lengths to disguise the manuscripts and smuggle them in small unnoticeable quantities out of the city under darkness. Working purely at night, the librarians loaded the manuscripts into small trunks and moved them by mule and camel to various safe houses. Using a network of agents and secret codes, manuscripts were ferried away under harrowing conditions. Agents had to learn to out-think al-Qaida and out-talk them when things got sticky. The public was not privileged to know the details of the operations for fear of being sold out. The agents knew each other and maintained a strict code of secrecy to safeguard each other. Ultimately, the badass Timbuktu librarians could smuggle 350,000 manuscripts to safety.

Today, they are safeguarded in secret locations around Mali and the surrounding areas. In time, the librarians hope to return the sacred text to its rightful home in Timbuktu. Now you know.

Chapter 10

Thomas Downing: The Black Oyster King of New York

In 1800s New York, Oyster dives were the absolute best place to find the best oysters. These rooms were located in a cellar and distinguished by the red lantern hanging outside the doors. A strict rule was that no women were allowed in these places unless they were a prostitute. What many people don't know about these popular American hideaways is that most of these joints were owned by African Americans.

There was one oyster dive that was the center of gravity. It was leaps and bounds above the rest, and it was owned by the best oyster bar owner ever to do it, Mr. Thomas Downing. Downing was born to parents who were once enslaved but were manumitted by their enslaver, John Downing. After gaining their freedom, the parents became the paid caretakers of the Downing property, allowing them to purchase some land for their children.

Their son Thomas joined the army and ended up in Philadelphia at the end of the War of 1812. Around this time, Thomas and his new wife Rebecca opened their first oyster joint. Downing moved to NY, where he once again established an oyster business on the street. To make a real profit, Thomas understood that he had to open his oyster dive, which had to be better than the existing ones.

The Thomas Downing Oyster House, ~~which was~~ quite upmarket and situated in the basement apartment at 5 Broad Street, opened its doors in 1825. Most of the downtown oyster dives were located in the African American neighborhood of Five Points, just a few blocks away from this beautiful site in the center of the business sector. The exquisite design was completed by damask curtains, gilt mirrors, and a brilliant chandelier. He added to his innovations by allowing wives as long as their husbands came along. Due to the business's success, Downing expanded to the nearby 3 and 7 Broad Street structures.

His mind allowed him to think globally, and Thomas started exporting oysters all over Europe, even to Queen Victoria herself. She was so impressed with his oysters that she shipped him a gold chronometer watch. Additionally, Downing shipped large quantities of oysters to the West Indies.

Despite the success of the Thomas Downing Oyster House, Downing spent ~~a lot of~~ much time advocating for the abolition of slavery. He was an Underground Railroad conductor and simultaneously ran a multinational oyster company. He founded the African Free School, where his five children attended for many years. He established the all-Black Anti-Slavery Society of the City of New York. He joined the Committee of Thirteen, an organization created to prevent free persons from being abducted and taken to the South, where they would be sold into slavery; in 1837, New York abolished slavery.

In 1838, he sued the New York trolley system after a driver assaulted him when he refused to get off the trolley. This was the beginning of a 20-year fight to desegregate the trolleys. On April 9th, 1866, the Civil Rights Act went into effect, declaring all male persons born in the United States citizens. Thomas Downing died on April 10th, 1866, meaning Thomas was only legally a citizen of the United States for one day. Now you know.

Chapter 11

Molly Williams: The First Black Female Firefighter

Firefighting has existed as long as man and fire have been together. Fire, one of the elements of the universe, refuses to be controlled, and man, the master of Earth, attempts to exploit it. These two entities have dueled each other for hundreds of thousands of years. Fires have done damage beyond quantification, and many have succumbed to the heat, flames, and smoke associated with fire. Even God Himself has promised to use the power of fire for his final act of wrath. Yet, as powerful as fire is, there was one recorded instance in which fire ran up against a worthy adversary in an unknown Black woman. This is her story.

In 1818 in New York City, the institution of slavery was alive and well. Although abolitionists were working hard to eliminate slavery from the state, some believed that Black Americans were born for a life of servitude.

Benjamin Aymar was a wealthy slaveholder in New York and a city merchant. He made his money in commercials selling goods, products, and people. He often cosplayed as a volunteer firefighter for

Oceanus Engine Company #11 in Lower Manhattan. Aymar had an enslaved Black woman he purchased to tend to him as he worked. Her name was Molly Williams.

As an enslaved woman, Molly had no say in the duties she was expected to perform. She often worked wherever Benjamin Aymar worked, including the firehouse. History says she worked as a cook at the firehouse and as a servant tending the needs of the men. Although relatively obscure and considered "just another negro slave," her legacy would forever change in 1818.

An influenza outbreak in the city decimated the number of men available for duty. Most firefighters and volunteers were sick and shut-in, unable to do the service of a firefighter. A massive fire broke out at what could only be described as the worst possible time. With members of the force out of commission, no one was left to fight a fire.

As a blizzard crippled the city in conjunction with a disease that disabled men, an urgent message came in about a blaze that had sprung up in the town. No man was available to answer the call, but a woman was available. Having repeatedly watched the firefighters get ready in their gear, Molly replicated what they did and put on the available clothing. Being alone and untrained, she mustered up unbelievable strength and single-handily hauled the pumper to the fire. With the courage of a lion and the calmness of a seasoned veteran, Molly primed the pumper and battled the blaze amid a raging blizzard. Finally, after both woman and fire engaged in combat, the fire died, and Molly emerged victorious.

For her actions that night, Molly earned the nickname Volunteer No. 11. FDNY didn't have a female firefighter for another 164 years, and that was only because several women won a discrimination suit against the city. Today, we recognize Molly Williams for blazing other Black female firefighters' paths. She not only combated the fire, but she also combated racism and prevailing notions of Black incompetence and female inferiority. She was once an enslaved woman; then, she became a legend. Now you know.

Chapter 12

The Power of "X." How Black People Used Their Signature to Fight Racism

In antebellum times, many Black people could not read and write due to laws that prevented them from learning. After the Civil War, four million former bondsmen were free and eligible to participate in the voting process. A considerable effort all across the South was in motion to get the negro registered, but there was one major complication; most were illiterate.

To combat this problem, the Freedman's Bureau wrote the names of Black people on the registrations, but the registration was only valid when signed by the registered person. Because the negro could not write their name, they were encouraged to substitute their signature with an "X."

Southern whites grew increasingly frustrated as the barriers they instilled were maneuvered around. Black people found ways to be resourceful and subvert the pathologies formed before them because of institutional racism. With this small but symbolic gesture, nearly four million Blacks entered the political arena to secure sociopolitical and economic interests for future generations. Even though they couldn't write their names, they signed their commitment to challenge prevailing notions of inferiority.

Even today, an X-mark signature is made by a person instead of an actual signature. Due to illiteracy or disability, a person may be unable to sign a full signature to a document as proof that its content has been reviewed and approved. To be legally valid, the X-mark signature must be witnessed. Next time you see an "X-mark signature" on antebellum documents, know that Black people may not have learned how to write their name, but they knew how to cast their vote for a better future. Now you know.

Chapter 13

Robert Johnson: The Man Who Sold His Soul to The Devil

Robert Leroy Johnson was a relatively unknown delta blues guitar player in the early 1900s. Yet, he's also remembered as an icon and a legend. He recorded 29 songs, and only three photographs of him exist. He lived a short life of tragedy juxtaposed against quick success…and sold his soul to the devil. (According to legend)

Robert was born out of wedlock. He never met his father at all. He had a terrible relationship with his stepfather, who wanted Robert to work the fields as a sharecropper. Robert was a decent harmonica player searching for his identity and independence. At age 19, he married 16-year-old Virginia Travis in 1929. She died just one year later, giving birth to their child. To say it mildly, Robert had a painful upbringing marked by tragedy and mental anguish.

Robert met legendary blues player Son House when House moved to where Robert was residing. Robert would listen to House and other players, eventually inspired to pick up the guitar. Robert had little success, and Son House and others would joke about how terrible Robert was as a guitar player. Others would chastise the legends for letting Robert pick up a guitar around them.

From 1932 until he died in 1938, Robert traveled frequently between cities attempting to gain notoriety and income as a blues player. When Robert returned to play alongside Son House and other legends, they were astounded at how good he was. In under two years, Robert had gone from a terrible novice to what other codes considered a master's master.

Legend has it that Robert had such a strong desire to become a master blues guitarist that he would do anything to achieve it. Robert received instructions to bring his guitar to a crosswalk near Dockery Plantation at midnight from an unidentified source. He reportedly reached the intersection of US 61 and US 49 in Clarksdale and dropped to his knees. He cried out in agony, a howl that rang through the night. A wail of helplessness, it was. One from fear, jealousy, and the ~~agony~~suffering of failure. He wasn't alone, ~~though~~however.

He claimed that a prominent Black man took his guitar, tuned it for him, and started playing a few tunes when he arrived. The deal was done when the stranger gave Robert his guitar back. Robert created the blues that would eventually make him a legend in exchange for his soul.

No one thought his rapid skill development could have resulted from simple repetition. Robert excelled as a guitarist playing the delta blues in just two years. After a random encounter at a crossroad at midnight, he outperformed icons who had spent their entire careers playing to learn how to perform the feats he could.

Giving one's soul to a spiritual being is not new in Black culture. For instance, Papa Legba is sometimes called the Lord of the Crossroads. Papa Legba has different functions within Haitian Vodou, such as the keeper of intersections, roads, doors, and so on. He acts as a liminal figure between the spirit and mortal worlds, able to communicate with both.

Robert died in 1938, at only 27 years old. (The famous 27-club starts with his death) There was no known cause of death, and no autopsy was performed. The exact location of Robert's burial is unknown, although three headstones are present in three different areas. Now you know.

Chapter 14

Outlawing Dunking: How Racism Stained the Game of Basketball

Who doesn't love a good dunk? Next to a thrilling buzzer beater to win the game, a monster jam is the most electrifying and imposing move a player can use. Although only worth two points, a dunk can send a message, swing the game's momentum, and propel a player into the pantheon of dunk gods. Most people have a favorite player, a favorite moment, and a favorite dunk. A dunk is ~~the single~~ one of the most efficient way~~s~~ to score in the game. Yet, as sexy and stylish as the dunk is, there was a time when racism permeated its ugly head into the game of basketball and altered its face. When the question was asked, "Who doesn't love a good dunk?" The answer was clearly, "racist whites." Here's the story of how dunking was outlawed from basketball.

As long as Black players have played the game of basketball, they have dunked the ball. This is because, early on, Black players realized the move's efficiency and were equipped with the athleticism to score in that manner. For white basketball players, the journey wasn't so natural.

The first dunk in organized sport happened in 1936. Joe Fortenberry, a 6-foot-8-inch Texan, introduced the dunk during the Berlin Olympics. Fortenberry captained the American squad on its way to winning the gold medal in the first Olympics to include basketball. The first credited dunk in an NCAA game goes to a 7-foot white kid named Bob Kurland, who accidentally dunked the ball. In a 1944 game where Oklahoma A&M Aggies took on Temple, Kurland got the ball under the rim and at first attempted to get the ball high over the rim for a sure layup. Instead, he ended up palming the ball for security as he placed it through the rim. Even he was surprised at the dunk and thought the basket would be waved off.

From the earliest integration of Blacks into the game of basketball, the dunk quickly became associated with "coloreds" and "negros" because Blacks were the ones who could do it most often and with a high degree of accuracy. Whites refused to acknowledge its artistry and skill, and many considered it an insult, going so far as to attempt to hurt those who tried to dunk intentionally. They quickly dismissed it as a stain on the game. University of Kansas basketball coach Phog Allen said that "dunking does not display skill-only height advantage."

The 1966 Texas Western team depicted in the movie "Glory Road" started five Black men who dunked all over Kentucky, the number one team in the country. Adolph Rupp, a stark racist, coached the Wildcats. Dunking became political after these Black kids embarrassed the epitome of basketball excellence in Kentucky. The "dunk" was a physical manifestation of Black Power on the court.

Because of racism, the NCAA banned the slam dunk before the 1967-1968 college season. In the organization's words, the dunk "was not a skillful shot." Although the NCAA would never publicly admit it, the dunk was primarily banned because of UCLA's Lew Alcindor. He was so efficient at scoring over his opponents by dunking that the league felt it gave Lew an advantage. Plus, Lew was Black, and he was utterly dominant.

The NCAA left the ban in place for ten years to bring high-flying Black men down below the rim where whites believed the game should be played. High-flyers like Julius Erving and David Thompson had to play their entire college careers below the rimedge. Whites feared that Blacks were taking over the sport of basketball, and banning dunking was one way they attempted to even the playing fields. Now you know.

Chapter 15

The Defenders: A Secret Militant Organization of Tuscaloosa, Alabama

In the pantheon of armed self-defense groups, familiar names like the Deacons of Defense and Justice, the Black Liberation Army, and The Black Panthers for Self-Defense ring loudly. Most of us are familiar with these organizations, their principals, and their exploits as they labored for the protection of negros battling the forces of white supremacy. We also know that many other groups are far less famous, more clandestine, and localized, yet just as effective as their well-known counterparts. Alabama had one such organization, and this is their story.

Tuscaloosa, Alabama, is fifty miles southwest of Birmingham and was a stronghold for Klan activity. 1956 after three years of court battles, the University of Alabama admitted Autherine Lucy as its first Black student. On her third day of college, a mob of hundreds of whites attacked her with the intent to kill her. She was rescued by a state policeman who drove her to the safety of other Blacks in the neighborhood who could ferry her away from the crowd. Shortly after this incident, Lucy was expelled from the University of Alabama because the school claimed it could not guarantee her safety. This single incident is the genesis of a clandestine militant organization built and sustained on armed self-defense.

Officially, the organization does not have a name, and very little is known about it due to its secrecy. Over time, some resorted to calling them, The Defenders. Yet, through oral history and some records, we know that the organization was founded by Joseph Mallisham, a native of Tuscaloosa and a Korean War veteran. He organized a group of Korean War vets and World War II vets. They were externally supported by local factory workers, teachers, businesspeople, and young gang leaders. They organized and structured the organization to resemble a military unity. The position of Commander chaired a small executive board that determined strategy, marshaled lieutenants, and organized troops. The requirements for membership were passing a background check to protect against infiltration, having seen combat in war, and a pledge to defend the Black community, even at the cost of one's own life. The organization did not accept heavy drinkers or those with a reputation for talking too much.

The group was unique in being secretive, yet it sometimes operated in full view of the white community. The group believed in armed self-defense, and each member was often heavily armed. The group was also unique in protecting white citizens who labored on behalf of negroes.

Before the group's founding, it had been a standard practice of the Ku Klux Klan to attend various meetings and intimidate and harass the local Black attendees. One day the Defenders showed up armed and ready to do violence, causing the KKK to scatter. The Klan never again openly showed up to another meeting. On another occasion, a mob of nearly 200 whites attacked a group of Black kids who attempted to go to the Druid movie theater. The teens managed to telephone the Defenders, and when they arrived, they found Klansman waiting. The KKK fired on the Defenders, and the Defenders fired back, laying down a barrage of intense and accurate gunfire. The Klan fled in shock and defeat. Klan violence in Tuscaloosa's Black community ended when Klansman discovered that attacks on Blacks would be met with an organized armed response.

The Defenders have faded into obscurity after their presence was felt. Not much else is known about them. What is certain is that this local clandestine organization believed in the concept of armed self-defense and deployed it with conviction, thereby shifting the tide of racial violence in Tuscaloosa, Alabama. Now you know.

Chapter 16

Pearls: A Story of Slavery, Women of Color, and Trade

For centuries, pearls have adorned people's necks, wrists, and clothing. Their history is expansive and deep. Today, pearls are often associated with femininity, grace, and wealth. Yet, there is a history of pearls that needs to be told. An account that is much darker and hidden from public discourse. The story of ~~p~~Pearl~~s~~ and ~~the level of~~ transatlantic slavery ~~are~~is intrinsically connected. The complex history of pearls is a history of slavery, geography, and commodity trade from one end of the globe to the other, often at the expense of exploiting people of color.

To understand the relationship between pearls and oppression, you must first understand where pearls were harvested. Places like Sri Lanka, Tuticorin, Baja California, and especially~~,~~ The Pearl Coast have the distinction of yielding most of the pearls from the early modern period. Additionally, pearls have often been gendered, said to have traits resembling a female. Pliny the Elder wrote of pearls, highlighting that pearls were believed to be the product of intercourse, while oysters were sensual, erotic, slippery, and reminiscent of female genitalia. Lastly, pearls have always been associated with the highest things (royalty, the heavens, virtuous women) and the lowest things (the darkness and the depths of the sea).

Shortly after the fall of the last Moorish kingdom on the Iberian Peninsula, the Catholic Monarchs were surrounded by the material expressions of Moorish wealth. Europeans had grown accustomed to seeing Moorish men and women wearing this precious jewel. The king and Queen of Spain drafted an agreement with Christopher Columbus that specified that a tenth of all particular things that Columbus discovered were granted to him, and the other nine parts were to be returned to Spain, especially pearls. It wasn't until Columbus's third voyage that he encountered pearls. Yet, it was an encounter that would forever change the landscape.

In a stretch of land labeled "The Pearl Coast," Spanish powers sought to enslave Caribbean peoples for pearl harvesting. In 1518, a new request asked the Spanish crown to provide black-skinned enslaved people directly from Africa to cultivate the pearls. This led to Pearl Coast residents paying slave traders for their human cargo in the same currency the enslaved would be expected to harvest pearls. The two industries—pearl harvesting and the transatlantic slave trade were deeply intertwined from their earliest days. Black divers would drive the pearl trade for the next 100-plus years, often dying in the sea or on the surface under the brutal system of slavery.

In contemporary times, pearls and Black women have a symbiotic relationship. Pearls are the ultimate symbol of strength, wisdom, refinement, integrity, and loyalty. Pearls have been the choice of jewelry for members of the Prince Hall Associate Order of the Eastern Star since 1874. The BGLO sororities are also connected to pearls, symbolizing founders or cardinal virtues. Pearls are created through pressure and roughness. Yet, the results are a beautiful jewel born from a hard beginning. Pearls came in various shapes, sizes, colors, and luster. Yet, they all have value to them. In many ways, pearls are a natural representation of Black women. From humble beginnings, cherished by all, sought after by many, highly respected, and valuable beyond measure, pearls, and Black women are intrinsically connected. Like Black women, pearls were harvested under oppression, traded for wealth, and prized. Much like pearls, Black women have endured the dark depths of the bottom, risen to the light, and emerged as one of the most sought-after things on this earth. The story of pearls is very much the story of Black women. Now you know.

Chapter 17

The Groveland Four: When White Women Lie

The cries and lies of white women have long resulted in the horrific deaths and abuse of Black people. No matter how improbable or fabricated these lies were, the consequences were devastating, and evil would be unleashed on individuals and entire towns in many cases. The pattern of white women's lies is a scholarship that many historians have documented with intense focus, yet it is as modern as it is historical. Unfortunately, that pattern still exists today. White women have been conditioned to understand that their lies are their primary weapon and defense mechanism. The story of the Groveland Four illustrates this point precisely.

On 16 July 1949, in a rural part of Florida known as Lake County, four young Black boys were falsely accused of raping 17-year-old Norma Padgett and assaulting her husband. The white teenager told police she and her husband were driving home from a dance when they were attacked by four young Black men who abducted and raped her at gunpoint. A mob quickly organized, and these white woman lies set off a search that spurred an onslaught of violence against Black residents of Groveland, ending in the deployment of the National Guard.

The four young boys were Ernest Thomas, 16-year-old Charles Greenlee, Samuel Shepherd, and Walter Irvin. Fearing a lynching by the mob, Ernest Thomas fled and was killed on July 26, 1949. A sheriff's posse of 1,000 white men shot Thomas over 400 times after being found asleep under a tree in the southern part of Madison County. Greenlee, Shepherd and Irvin were arrested. They were beaten severely to force confessions, but Irvin refused to confess. The three survivors were convicted at trial by an all-white jury. Greenlee was sentenced to life because he was only 16 at the time of the alleged crime; the other two were sentenced to death.

The NAACP took the case to represent the boys, with Thurgood Marshall leading the defense. In 1951, the U.S. Supreme Court ordered a retrial after hearing the appeals of Shepherd and Irvin. It ruled they had not received a fair trial because no evidence had been presented, because of excessive adverse publicity, and because Bblack people had been excluded from the jury. The court overturned the convictions and remanded the case to the lower court for a new trial.

In November 1951, Sheriff Willis V. McCall of Lake County, Florida, shot Irvin and Shepherd while they were in his custody and handcuffed together. McCall claimed they had tried to escape while he was transporting them from Raiford State Prison back to the county seat of Tavares for the new trial. Shepherd died on the spot; Irvin survived and later told FBI investigators that McCall had shot them in cold blood and that his deputy, Yates, had also shot him in an attempt to kill him. Harry Moore, executive director of the Florida NAACP, called for the Governor of Florida to suspend McCall. On Christmas Night, 1951, a bomb went below Moore's house, fatally wounding him and his wife; he died that night, and his wife followed nine days later. The bombers were never caught.

At the second trial, Marshall represented Irvin, again convicted by an all-white jury and sentenced to death. In 1955, his death sentence was commuted to life in prison by recently elected Governor LeRoy Collins. He was paroled in 1968 but died the following year in Lake County, purportedly of natural causes. Greenlee was paroled in 1962 and lived with his family until he died in 2012. In 2016, the City of Groveland and Lake County each apologized to the survivors of the four men for the injustice against them.

Norma Padgett, the white woman who initially lied to the four boys, is still alive as of 2023. Now you know.

Chapter 18

African American Black Heritage and the Juneteenth Flag

The Black American Heritage Flag had its genesis in March of 1967 and was created by Melvin Charles and Gleason T. Jackson. The idea was born out of a need for flag representation. Charles and Jackson noticed that other ethnic groups had flags representing their heritage, yet Black Americans had no such model. The men felt a flag should exist that symbolized the Black Culture that was created in America after the Atlantic Slave Trade that took place between the 16th and 19th centuries.

Charles and Jackson created a design representing resilience, power, and unity and the time and love that went into developing America's Black culture. The method of the flag is ripe with meaningful illustration, and here is what it represents.

The details are one diagonal black stripe centered between two red lines. Superimposed on the black stripe is a blunted Moorish sword surrounded by a golden wreath of fig leaves. The sword harkens back to the Moorish leaders of the 8th century and represents the strength and authority exhibited by a Black culture that made many contributions to the world. The wreath of fig leaves represents the sustainment of life even under unimaginable conditions. The cultivated fig, native to Africa, is one of the most ancient life-sustaining fruits. Red means the blood shed by African Americans for freedom and equality in America. The color black represents pride in the black race. The color gold represents intellect, prosperity, and peace.

Ben Haith, an activist and the man behind the National Juneteenth Celebration Foundation (NJCF), is the creator of the original Juneteenth Flag. Haith and his coworkers designed the flag in 1997, and Boston-based painter Lisa Jeanne Graf brought their idea to life. The flag was changed into the version we see today in 2000, claims the National Juneteenth Observance Foundation. The date "June 19, 1865" was added seven years later to honor when Union Army Major General Gordon Granger rode into Galveston, Texas, and informed enslaved African Americans of their freedom.

~~we know today. Seven years later, the date "June 19, 1865" was added, commemorating the day that Union Army Maj. Gen. Gordon Granger rode into Galveston, Texas, and told enslaved African Americans of their emancipation.~~

According to Haith, designing the flag and its symbols was a deliberate process. Here are their meanings. Haith said the white star in the flag's center has a dual purpose. For one, it represents Texas, the Lone Star State. It was in Galveston in 1865 that Union soldiers informed the country's last remaining enslaved people that, under the Emancipation Proclamation issued two years earlier, they were free. But the star also goes beyond Texas, representing the freedom of African Americans in all 50 states. The bursting outline around the star is inspired by a nova, a term astronomers use to mean a new star.

The Juneteenth flag represents a new beginning for the African Americans of Galveston and throughout the land. The curve extending across the flag's width represents a new horizon: the opportunities and promises ahead for Black Americans. The red, white, and blue represent the American flag, a reminder that enslaved people and their descendants were and are Americans. June 19, 1865, represents the day enslaved Black people in Galveston, Texas, became Americans under the law. Now you know.

Chapter 19

Cat-Hauling: A Cruel and Unusual Punishment

Slave narratives and the personal diaries of enslavers provide the clearest examples of the horrors the enslaved endured at the foot of bondage. Historians have dug deep to catalog the various methods of punishment and oppression on the plantations. Most of us are familiar with what can be described as "typical" punishments.

These are whippings with a cowhide whip or a cat-o-nine-tails. The cowhide whip was the most common whip used by overseers. The cat-o-nine-tails was a whip that had nine leather straps coming off of it. Often the ends of the letter straps would be adorned with bones or seashells. This caused the shells to cleave to the flesh and rip it clean. Another method of punishment was the "salt bath," where a victim was beaten bloody and then doused in salt, causing excruciating pain. Other methods of torture we're familiar with are branding, sexual penetration in the form of rape, buck-breaking, and being put in the "hot box" for several days. Sometimes the enslaved were loaded with heavy items to cause excruciating pain. Sometimes the bonds people were stripped naked to shame them

There is one form of torturous punishment that many of us are less familiar with, and it is known as cat-hauling. It is described as when an overseer would force a ~~bond~~bond person to lie flat on their stomach and fasten them down with their arms and legs outstretched. Then they would place a cat on the person's back. Then they would drag the cat down that person's back by the tail. Naturally, the cat would eject its claws for stability, and those claws would rake a person's skin wide open. The probability of infection was extremely high, and the flesh was usually poisoned after the ordeal. Often the cat-hauling ordeal was followed by a salt bath.

This account comes from Charles Ball's slave narrative, *A Narrative of the Life and Adventures of Charles Ball, a Black Man.* Theodore Dwight Weld's *American Slavery as It Is* (1844) explains that many enslaved persons considered cat-hauling crueler than lashing.

One planted wrote in his diary that whipping the negro had become dull and exhausting. He needed to find more creative ways to punish them. Unfortunately, the boredom and exertion of energy caused whites to find new and even more unusual ways to desecrate Black bodies. Here is how cat-hauling was described by those who witnessed it.

"A boy was then ordered to get up, run to the house, and bring a cat, which was soon produced. The large gray tomcat was then taken by the well-dressed gentleman and placed upon the bare back of the prostrate black man, near the shoulder, and forcibly dragged by the tail down the back and along the bare thighs of the sufferer. The cat sunk his nails into the flesh and tore off pieces of the skin with his teeth. The man roared with the pain of this punishment and would have rolled along the ground had he not been held in his place by the force of four other enslaved people, each confined to a hand or a foot. As soon as the cat was drawn from him, the man said he would tell who stole the hog and confessed that he and several others, three of whom were holding him, had stolen the hog–killed, dressed, and eaten it."

The confession again drew the same punishment, with the cat dragged in the opposite direction this time, for the confessor and once in each order for his accomplices, who were all bathed in saltwater. In the pantheon of cruel and usual punishment endured by the enslaved Blacks in America, cat-hauling is another example of the heinous activity the slaver deals with. Now you know.

Chapter 20

The Kissing Case of 1958: Childs Play and the Consequences of White Lies

The interactions between Bblack men and white women have yielded some of the evilest reactions in the history of humanity. From physical violence, incarceration, and brutal deaths, the consequences of white women pointing at Black men are from the devil himself. History has tried diligently to record these consequences to expose a pattern of falsehoods and lies, leading to the deaths and violations of thousands upon thousands of Black men. But what happens when it's just children involved? One would think that evil and brutality would be eliminated from the consequences. Yet, history shows us this is not true. The case of George Stinney, the 14-year-old Black boy executed via the electric chair in South Carolina, is an example of the wide arching range of evil and racism regarding white females and Black male interactions. Here is but another example.

In October 1958, in Monroe, North Carolina, Sissy Marcus, an 8-year-old white female child, told her mother she had kissed 9-year-old James "Hanover" Thompson, and 7-year-old David "Fuzzy" Simpson, on their cheeks. Both boys were Negro. She had seen them while with other children and recognized James as a friend. The two had played together when James joined his mother at her job as a domestic for the Marcus family.

When Sissy told her mother, Bernice Marcus, about the encounter, the woman became enraged and washed her daughter's mouth with lye. She called the police and accused the boys of raping her daughter. Her husband, Sissy's father, and neighbors picked up shotguns and went looking for the boys and their parents.

Local officials unlawfully detained the two young boys, who were arrested in October 1958 and refused to allow them to see their parents or legal counsel for a week. Police beat the boys and threatened them with more injury to extract confessions. After being jailed for three months, the boys were charged by Juvenile Judge Hampton Price and convicted of molestation. The judge based his guilty verdict on the fact that the boys stayed silent and would not confess, even under torture. Price sentenced them to reform school until the age of 21.

The boys were imprisoned in the North Carolina State Reformatory in October 1958. The National Office of the NAACP refused to take the case citing their policy of not taking cases involving "sexual abuse." The local chapter, headed by President Robert F. Williams, raised funds to hire noted civil rights lawyer Conrad Lynn from New York. The boy's mothers had been fired from their domestic jobs, and the NAACP relocated them to nearby towns for safety.

The case was considered such a gross abuse of authority and inaccuracies that former First Lady Eleanor Roosevelt tried to reason with the North Carolina governor. The boys were kept from their mothers for weeks until Joyce Egginton, a journalist from London, got permission to visit the boys and brought the mothers along. She also smuggled in a camera and photographed the boys who showed apparent signs of torture and starvation. The photographs ran in media throughout Europe and Asia, causing international embarrassment to the United States. Demonstrations in support of the boys were held as far away as Paris, Rome, Vienna, and Rotterdam.

After the boys had spent three months in detention and bowing to global pressure, the governor pardoned Thompson and Simpson without conditions or explanation. The state and city never apologized to the boys or their families for their treatment. Now you know.

Chapter 21

Major Taylor: The Man Who Searched for a Rival and Never Found One

  The sport of cycling is trendy today within the Black community. Many predominantly Black bike clubs across the country promote the sport of cycling and share in the camaraderie and the spirit of competition. Although the sport is more popular today than yesteryear, the history of the sport still needs to be developed. Black cyclists are riding on the legacy of perhaps the most significant Black cyclist in the sport. This is his story.

  He was born Marshall Walter "Major" Taylor from Indianapolis. He learned about bikes by working in a bicycle shop and competing in local races. He moved to Worcester, Massachusetts, with his coach in his teenage years. At this stage, he had a masterful amateur career where he honed his skills, proliferated, and began to break records back-to-back.

  In 1896, Major turned professional at the tender age of 18. In 1897, he streamlined his focus to the sprint event and began competing on the national circuit. In the following years, he smashed several world records in races ranging from the quarter mile to the two-mile sprint.

In 1899, Major won the 1-mile sprint event at the 1899 world track championships to become the first African American to achieve the level of cycling world champion and the second Bblack athlete to win a world championship in any sport, following Canadian boxer George Dixon of 1890. Major was also a national sprint champion in 1899 and 1900. During 1898–99, at the peak of his cycling career, Taylor established seven world records. He raced in the U.S., Europe, and Australia from 1901 to 1904, beating the world's best riders. After a 2.5-year hiatus, he returned in 1907–1909 before retiring at age 32 to his home in Worcester in 1910.

In the early years of his professional racing career, Taylor's reputation increased as he competed in and won more races. Newspapers began referring to him as the "Worcester Whirlwind," the "Black Cyclone," the "Ebony Flyer," the "Colored Cyclone," and the "Black Zimmerman," among other nicknames. He also gained popularity among the spectators. One of his fans was President Theodore Roosevelt, who kept track of Taylor throughout his seventeen-year racing career.

Despite all the accomplishments in the face of insurmountable odds, Major faced extreme, often violent racism in this predominantly white sport. In 1893, after 15-year-old Taylor beat a one-mile amateur track record, he was verbally harassed and barred from the track. Major was locked out of the significant cycling clubs, which helped to influence his decision to join the See-Saw Cycling Club, which was formed by black cyclists of Indianapolis who could not enter the local all-white Zigzag Cycling Club.

In November and December 1897, when the circuit extended to the racially segregated South, local race promoters refused to let Taylor compete because he was Bblack. While some of Taylor's fellow racers declined to compete with him, others resorted to intimidation, verbal insults, and threats to harm him physically. Taylor recalled that ice water had been thrown at him during races, and nails were scattered in front of his wheels. In February 1904, when Taylor was competing in Australia, he was seriously injured on the final turn of a race when fellow competitor Iver Lawson veered his bicycle toward Taylor and collided with his front wheel. Taylor crashed and lay unconscious on the track before he was taken to a local hospital and later fully recovered.

Nearly twenty years after retirement, Taylor wrote and self-published his autobiography, *The Fastest Bicycle Rider in the World: The Story of a Colored Boy's Indomitable Courage and Success Against Great Odds: An Autobiography.*

In March 1932, Taylor suffered a heart attack and was hospitalized in the Provident Hospital. He died on June 21, at age 53. His wife and daughter, who survived him, did not immediately learn of his death, and no one claimed his remains. He was initially buried at Mount Glenwood Cemetery in Thornton Township, Cook County, near Chicago, in an unmarked pauper's grave. Eventually, his body was exhumed and reburied in a more prominent location at the cemetery. Now you know.

Chapter 22

Queen Charlotte of Mecklenburg: The Black Royal

Charlotte, NC, is one of the most beautiful cities in America. It is undoubtedly one of the fastest growing cities, and that is because of its opportunity, star power, and potential—those in the Carolinas known Charlotte as The Queen City. Many outside the city don't know that the city is named after Queen Sophia Charlotte of Mecklenburg-Strelitz on the British throne. What is even less known than that is that Queen Charlotte was infused with Black blood. Of course, an army of people is ready to defend the purity of Queen Charlotte's blood, void of any Black infusion. Yet, the truth doesn't need anyone to believe it for it to be the truth. Here's what the evidence suggests.

Queen Charlotte was from Germany and became the wife of the English King George III. She was a direct descendant of Margarita de Castro y Sousa, a Portuguese royal house Black branch. The first evidence is found in the portraits. It was customary for artists to downplay any African features of people of mix-raced nobility. This is to hide their African look and replace it with European-like features.

Queen Charlotte's prominent African characteristics had political significance in many of her portraits.

Sir Allan Ramsay was the artist responsible for most of the paintings of the queen, and his representations of her were the most decidedly African of all her portraits. Sir Allen Ramsay was also very anti-slavery, and this viewpoint was well known. He also married the niece of Lord Mansfield, the English judge whose 1772 decision was the first in a series of rulings ending slavery in the British Empire. Therefore, the evidence strongly suggests that Sir Allen Ramsey was anti-slavery and pro-Moor. Because of his pro-Black stance, Sir Allen Ramsey refused to hide any of Queen Charlotte's African features in the portraits of her that he painted.

According to the diary of Baron Stockmar, he described Charlotte as "small and crooked, with a real Mulatto face." According to Horace Walpole, the 4th Earl of Oxford, English writer and historian, he described Queen Charlotte as "nostrils spreading too wide; mouth has the same fault."

In the American Colonies, the slogan: "the Queen of England was a Negro woman" was weaponized by the British Vice Admiral, Sir Alexander Cochrane, in his campaign to persuade enslaved people to defect to the British during the War of 1812. More than 4,000 n~~N~~egros joined with British forces, making it the largest emancipation in the US until the Civil War.

Proponents and critics of Queen Charlotte's African ancestry will point to her line of origin from a Moorish woman named Madregana, the Black mistress of King Afonso III of Portugal. To believers, this is the descendant whose African blood Charlotte has in her and the reason for her African features. To critics, they argue that anyone who was 15 generations removed would be too diluted to have any effect on Queen Charlotte's appearance.

In 2017 following the announcement of Prince Harry and Meghan Markle's engagement, several news articles were published promoting the claims of Queen Charlotte being Black. David Buck, a Buckingham Palace spokesperson, was quoted by the *Boston Globe* as saying: "This has been rumored for years and years. It is a matter of history; frankly, we've got far more important things to discuss." Now you know.

Chapter 23

Tippu Tip: The Most Prolific Slave Trader of All-Time

Slavery in Africa has a history that will be a part of the story of humanity for time immortal. From Barbary slavery to Romans to Trans-Atlantic to the Arab slave trade and beyond, Africa has had its share of slavery in various forms and capacities stretching across the full girth of the continent. Of the millions upon millions of Africans who have been plundered and sold into bondage by traders, one man singlehandedly outpaced any other slave trader in the history of Africa. That man is known as Tippu Tip.

Hamad ibn Muhammed al Murjebi was his birth name. History would remember him as Tippu Tip. Tippu was born between 1832-1837 in Zanzibar. He was the son of an Arab slave trader and an African mother. In his early years, he led a group of about 100 men into Central Africa to plunder enslaved people and ivory.

In the 19th century, the scale of trade on the Swahili Coast rose tremendously. In the late 19th century, Zanzibar became the most prosperous port on the East Coast of Africa. Annual trade, adjusted for inflation today, was equivalent to $100M. The demand for ivory grew to a feverish pitch, and the desire for this commodity came from as far away as Europe and America. It's estimated that ivory traders slaughtered 17,000 elephants a year for their tusks.

The man who had the most control over the trade of ivory was Tippu Tip. At the height of his empire, he controlled a region totaling 250,000 square miles. Tippu bought ivory from the interior to transport it to the coastal trade ports. By the 1880s, Tip controlled a territory the size of California.

The trade networks ran from one side of Africa to the other, directly through the Lunda and Luba empire of central Africa. Tippu took advantage of this to move his product, reaping huge profits. While hunting elephants for ivory, Tippu's men also plundered towns and villages for supplies and enslaved people. The enslaved people would then become the vessels to move massive quantities of ivory to the ports. Once at the port, the enslaved people would be sold off in the booming slave economy of Zanzibar for enormous profits.

After the Berlin Conference, between 1884 and 1885, Tip claimed the Eastern Congo for himself and the Sultan of Zanzibar. When, in August 1886, fighting broke out between the Swahili and the representatives of King Leopold II of Belgium, Tip went to the Belgian consul at Zanzibar to assure him of his "good intentions." Because of this, King Leopold II advocated for Tippu to become the governor of a new district in the Congo Free State called Stanley Falls.

By 1895, Tippu had acquired seven plantations and had 10,000 slaves of his own. In the 19th century, 1.6 million enslaved people were shipped out of East Africa. That's 4X the amount of enslaved people sent out of Africa directly to the United States. An estimated 70,000 Africans a year were brought to Zanzibar by Tippu Tip. Tippu is directly responsible for putting over 1M Africans into bondage.

Historian and Scholar Dr. Henry Louis Gates is quoted as having said, "He was as notoriously brutal and evil as any white slave trader. I have absolutely no doubt that if there's a hell, Tippu Tip is in it." Now you know.

Chapter 24

The Kushites and The Black Pharaoh Who Brought Egypt to Her Knees

Suppose I ask you to name a tremendously advanced African civilization, full of cultural charisma and ancient iconography, with incredible statues, pyramids, artwork, and pharaohs. In that case, you'd most likely say, "Egypt." You wouldn't be wrong, but you'd probably struggle if I asked you to name one not called Egypt. This is what the Egyptians wanted. To erase the historical legacy of the mighty Kushites, a subordinate people who rose to conquer their conquerors and rule Egypt.

The Kushites originated south of Egypt in ancient Kush, which is now Sudan. They were also builders, warriors, and gold miners. The Kushites are now almost completely forgotten because of the color of their skin. Egyptians also called the area Ta-Nehsy, Latin for "Land of the Black People." Greek and Roman authors referred to the region as Aethiopia (Land of the Burnt-Faced Persons) because of the native population's dark skin tone and Arab tribes referred to it as Bilad al-Sudan (Land of the Blacks) because of their dark skin tones.

The Kushites and the Egyptians have a lengthy and extensive history together. In Kerma's historic center is a temple called Deffufa, which served as a place of worship for the ancient Kushites. It was one of the first still-standing African buildings to be built at the same time as the Egyptian pyramids.

Egypt and Kush were equal in intelligence and technological prowess. Trade was the foundation of their tight ties. The most important of the many traded commodities was gold. Despite their love of gold, it wasn't made in Egypt. It was first mined in Kush by powerful gold miners. Nubia was referred to as "the land of gold." ~~In terms of intelligence and technology, Egypt and Kush were on par. Their close ties were built on trade. Gold was the most significant of the many exchanged commodities. Although they were fond of gold, it didn't originate in Egypt. It originated in Kush, where strong gold miners mined it. It was said that Nubia was "the land of gold."~~

When fighting between the Kushites and the Egyptians started, Egypt reacted physically and started a propaganda effort to discredit the Kushites. Egyptians call Kush "wretched Kush" and "vile Kush." In depictions, Kushites were beaten to death by the pharaoh or tied and shackled beneath the king's feet. Kushites were referred to as "savage" and "barbarous" by Egyptians, who started to "racially profile" them. This racial profiling exercise supported Egypt's case for annexing Kush in 1500. The Kushites' extraordinarily black skin helped set them apart from the Egyptians, whose brown skin is the color we now associate with historical individuals. ~~In addition to a physical response when conflict broke out between the Kushites and the Egyptians, Egypt also~~

~~launched an anti-propaganda campaign to demonize the Kushites. Kush is referred to as "wretched Kush" and "vile Kush" by Egyptians. In depictions, Kushites were tied and bound beneath the king's feet, or the pharaoh beat them to death. Kushites were labeled as "savage" and "barbarous" by Egyptians, who began to "racially profile" them. This racial profiling operation justified Egypt's justification for annexing Kush in 1500. The Kushites' extremely black skin helped distinguish them from the Egyptians' brown skin, which is how we currently depict historical figures with their skin tones.~~

<u>The Kushites joined Kemet as a vassal state after being vanquished by the Egyptians. The Kushite culture was influenced by Egypt, as evidenced by the pyramids built in Kush by the Kushite people. (Today, Sudan has more pyramids still standing than Egypt.) To survive being subjugated by Egypt, the Kushites had to imitate Egyptian culture. For 300 years, Egypt ruled over the Kushites. Egypt left Kush in 700 BC. Libyan warlords engaged in combat over who would rule the North. The Amun-Rah priest made an effort to keep the South united. Egypt sought the most improbable group of rescuers due to this unrest—the Kushites.</u>~~When the Egyptians defeated the Kushites, they became a~~

~~subordinate state of Kemet. Egyptian influence seeped into Kushite culture, where we see Kushites erecting pyramids in Kush. (Today, Sudan has more remaining pyramids than Egypt) The Kushites had to adopt Egyptian culture to survive being conquered by Egypt. Egypt ruled the Kushites for 300 years. In 700 BC, Egypt withdrew from Kush. Warlords from Libya fought for control of the North. The priest of the cult of Amun-Rah tried to hold the South together. Because of this turmoil, Egypt turned to the most unlikely rescuer imaginable…the Kushites.~~

<u>Piankhi, a young Kushite ruler, vowed to help those in need because he believed Amun-Rah had his back. His army routed foes at Thebes and further north into Memphis. Piankhi and his offspring started the 25th dynasty of Egypt. They controlled all the land and wealth from the Kush to the Mediterranean Sea. Amun gives Piankhi the red crown of lower Egypt and the white crown of higher Egypt, as depicted on the temple walls, uniting Egypt under a powerful Black king.</u> ~~A young Kushite monarch named Piankhi swore to assist those in need because he thought Amun-Rah had his back. At Thebes and further north into Memphis, his army defeated adversaries. Piankhi and his~~

98   History has its eyes on you

~~descendants founded Egypt's 25th dynasty. They ruled over all the land and wealth from the Kush to the Mediterranean Sea. Amun unites Egypt under a strong "black" pharaoh by giving Piankhi the red crown of lower Egypt and the white crown of higher Egypt, as seen on the walls of temples.~~

In 700 BC, the Kushite Pharaoh Taharqa stopped the Assyrians from destroying King Solomon's temple and Jerusalem. Pharaoh Taharqa is still regarded highly by Jews for doing this. ~~The Kushite Pharaoh Taharqa prevented the Assyrians from destroying Jerusalem and King Solomon's temple in 700 BC. Jews still hold Pharaoh Taharqa in high regard for doing this.~~

Pharaoh Psammeticus II of Egypt attacked Kush in 593 BC. Since a Kushite pharaoh had killed his grandpa, he wanted revenge. He had Kush in mind to forget. He demolished every statue, temple, and monument he could locate. History is continuously being changed now. The list of dynasties on the façade of the Egyptian Museum in Cairo only has one dynasty missing—the 25th dynasty of the Kushites. ~~Egypt launched an assault on Kush in 593 BC under Pharaoh Psammeticus II.~~

~~He desired retribution since a Kushite pharaoh had killed his grandfather. He intended to forget Kush. Every statue, temple, and monument he could find was destroyed. Even today, history is still being revised. Only one dynasty, the Kushites' 25th dynasty, is absent from the list of dynasties on the exterior of the Egyptian Museum in Cairo.~~

Africans with varied shades of brown skin comprised the Egyptian population throughout the dynasties. They had a solid grasp of color theory and applied it effectively in the paintings that adorned their walls. They employed colors ranging from light brown to dark brown to symbolize themselves. However, they purposefully used dark, nearly black ink when they drew the Kushites. This one motion shows how adeptly the Egyptians distinguished between different skin tones. ~~Over the dynasties, brown-skinned Africans of various hues made up the Egyptians. They had a good understanding of color theory and used it to significant effect in the paintings on their walls. When representing themselves, they used light brown to dark-brown pigment. However, they consciously used dark, almost black ink while drawing the Kushites. This action alone demonstrates how well the Egyptians recognized the variations in skin tones.~~

Even though the Black Pharaohs of Kush and the 25th dynasty period only reigned for 100 years, they could overthrow the Great Egyptian kingdom that had previously ruled over them. The Egyptians and Western education wiped the powerful Kushites out of history. American education was dominated by Eurocentric ideas, and Egypt and Kush wanted you to be ignorant of their cultures. Now you know.

Chapter 25

The Greatest Clarinet Player Ever. That's It. That's the Whole Title

New Orleans is one of the most fascinating cities on earth. It is the epicenter of music, art, food, and history. Here, African, European, and Spanish amalgamate to create the unmatched Creole and Cajun cultural buffet. Among the many beauties of New Orleans is its music. The city birthed jazz and germinated brass bands into the staples they are today. So many impressive people sit among the pantheon of musicians, and the names read like a roll call of superstar talents. There is Trombone Shorty, Louis Armstrong, Allen Toussaint, Kermit Ruffins, Fats Domino, the Hot-8 Brass Band, and many, many others. Yet, one name is so important and precious to the culture that it is destined to illuminate the hall of musicians for time immortal. That name is Doreen Ketchens.

Those of us who have had the pleasure of hearing the talent of Doreen's lives are witnesses to her magic and can attest to her remarkable abilities. For those who may not have experienced her in person, perhaps you've seen Doreen perform at some embassies for dignitaries. If not there, maybe you've seen her performing in a concert hall with a world-renowned orchestra. To go further, perhaps you have seen her performing for Presidents Carter, Reagan, Clinton, and Bush Sr. If you have not seen her performing at any of those venues, you can always return to the roots and find her in the French Quarters of New Orleans. You cannot often find the greatest of something performing for free right on the street for all to enjoy.

Doreen is known as The Clarinet Queen because of her high skill level and massive accomplishments. Ketchens began her journey in the New Orleans neighborhood of Treme, much like many others whose legendary skills have become associated with the New Orleans culture. She's a product of Southern University, among the institutes of higher learning she's attended.

Doreen started performing on the streets of New Orleans in 1987. From there, she's performed in Africa, Asia, Canada, Europe, South America, and Russia. She's been the subject of numerous documentaries, and she's also put out 21 albums. She's performed for presidents, dignitaries, royalty, and various governments. Yet, on any given day, you can find the greatest clarinet player ever playing to a crowd on the streets of the French Quarters in New Orleans. Now you know.

Chapter 26

Brothers In and Out of Bondage. An Examination of Free Blacks Who Enslaved People

When someone brings up the subject of Blacks in America owning other Blacks as enslaved peoples, it solicits a wide range of responses. For some, the answer is complete denial. It is simply unfathomable to accept the idea that Blacks would regulate other Blacks to bondage in America at a time when bondage was the worse condition possible. Different responses are that of acceptance but with a disclaimer. The argument is made that Blacks didn't enslave people; instead, they had indentured servants, which significantly differed from the condition of chattel slavery—some present slavery as philanthropy and a sense of protection from free Blacks to enslaved Blacks. Furthermore, the talking point that Blacks held other Blacks in bondage is an oversaturated talking point espoused by racists to help justify their racism and bias.

We must first address the truth. Yes, Free Blacks did enslave other Blacks. Primary sources such as census records, manumission records, and diaries prove the numbers of Free Black enslavers and the number of Black enslaved owned by them. Still, some don't know this historical fact. For instance, the great intellectual Booker T. Washington said, "My own personal recollections bring no case in the mind of free Black men owning spaces, nor am I able to refer you to any books referring to this phase of slavery, in the event it did exist." Yet, free Blacks enslaved people in the thirteen original states and later in every state that countenanced slavery.

Blacks became enslavers early in American history. In 1654 Anthony Johnson and his wife Mary won a court case in which they gained the services of their Black servant, John Casor, for life. According to author R. Halliburton, there were Black slaveholders in Boston as early as 1724, Connecticut by 1783, and Alabama by 1797. Among the earliest records in the "deed books" of St. Augustine, Florida, is a document recording the sale of an enslaved Black person to a free Black by a free Black. By 1790 forty-eight Maryland Black owners possessed 143 enslaved people. Nat Butler, a free Black who lived near Aberdeen in Harford County, owned a small farm and regularly purchased and sold negroes for the Southern trade.

According to several historical sources, free Black owners treated their enslaved people with equal or greater severity than white owners did. Due to their experience as freed indentured servants, black people became enslavers. Some people bought their freedom. Some people were born free by miscegenation, while others were taken to free parents. Black owners acquired enslaved people through gifts, purchases of other Blacks, and inheritance from White and Black relatives. ~~Some historical accounts considered free Black owners as severe or more severe on their slaves than white owners. Blacks became enslavers by way of being indentured servants who became free. Some purchased their freedom. Others were born of free parents, while some were born free by miscegenation. Black owners obtained enslaved people by inheritance through white and Black relatives, by way of gifts, and by purchasing other Blacks.~~

According to writers like U.B. Phillips, a tiny percentage of free Black enslavers purchased enslaved Black people for charitable purposes and were shielding their relatives who had been purchased as enslaved people to prevent them from being sold into slavery by whites. Kenneth Stampp advances that claim by claiming that Black enslavers bought spouses, wives, or kids who were not eligible for emancipation under the law at the time. According to author Luther Porter Jackson, enslaved persons were frequently manumitted, and free Black slave ownership was only ever transient. ~~Authors like U.B. Phillips argue that a small minority of free Black enslavers acquired enslaved Black people for benevolent reasons and were protecting their kin who were bought to keep them from being enslaved by whites. Kenneth Stampp furthers that argument by asserting that Black enslavers purchased husbands, wives, or children who could not emancipate under existing laws. Author Luther Porter Jackson argues that free Black slave ownership was temporary, and enslaved people were often manumitted.~~

What we know is that there were free Blacks who engaged in the practice of enslaving other Blacks. Census data from 1830 shows that the South and border states were home to 3,690 Black owners and 12,601 enslaved people. Whether it was for economic stratification, much like their white counterparts, or for benevolent reasons of protection and family gathering, Blacks engaged in slavery. Understanding the significance of history and excavating archives for authentic data is essential. By doing so, we reveal and begin to understand the severely underdeveloped scholarship of the antebellum South. Now you know.

History has its eyes on you

Chapter 27

Mac and Cheese: How an American Classic had its roots in Blackness

Macaroni and cheese is a trendy, classic American dish due to its flexibility and range. Whether it be a typical evening ~~dinner~~dinner or an extensive holiday buffet, mac and cheese is often one of the most requested dishes. Its popularity transcends class and race as it is found on the plates of the proletariat and the bourgeois, Black and white alike. Due to its simplicity and range, the dish is essential in the Black community's pantheon of African American cuisines. Its value cannot be underscored as it is found everywhere from pop culture, i.e., that thang sound like mac and cheese noises, to competitions at holiday tables among the self-proclaimed best cooks of the family. As much as the Black community loves mac and cheese, many of us are less familiar with its Black legacy. Here's its story.

Mac and c~~C~~heese come from 14th-century Italy. Most biased historians seek to attribute the story of mac and cheese in America to President Thomas Jefferson. Yet, Thomas Jefferson was not a cook. He was, in fact, a world traveler and a prolific enslaver. Of the over 600 bonds people that Thomas Jefferson owned, one of them was his mistress, Sally Hemings. Sally Hemings had a brother named James Hemings, who came to be the property of President Jefferson at eight years old.

James Hemings and his brother Robert were taken to Williamsburg and Richmond as personal attendants to Thomas Jefferson as teenagers. According to a letter from Jefferson to William Short dated 7 May 1784, it was the idea of Thomas Jefferson to take James Heming with him to France for culinary training. They all set sail from Boston Harbor on the 5th of ~~July,~~ July, 1784.

While in Paris, James Hemings was trained in French cooking. He studied first with the caterer and restaurateur, Monsieur Combeaux, apprenticed with pastry chefs, and then with a cook in the household of the Prince de Condé. After three years of study, he became the head chef at the Hôtel de Langeac, Jefferson's residence that also functioned as the American embassy. Here his dishes were served to international guests, politicians, authors, scientists, and European aristocrats.

After five years, James Hemings left Paris with Thomas Jefferson in October 1789 and returned to the United States as an enslaved man. Thomas Jefferson became extremely fond of a dish in

Paris consisting of pasta, macaroni, and cheese and wanted to continue to enjoy that dish back in the colonies. At the time, it was known as "pie called macaroni." By 1793, Jefferson was paying duty tax on imported macaroni, according to his mMemorandum books. Additionally, James Hemings improved the dish with available cheese, adding his culinary skills to enhance its taste and texture. In short, he addedsaid some culture to it.

Before James Hemings was manumitted, he was ordered to teach his younger brother Peter Hemings his culinary skills, especially the macaroni pie recipe. After James Hemings left Monticello, Peter Hemings was the head cook.

Peter Hemings further perfected the dish and taught it to another apprentice, Edith Hern Fossett, at Monticello. In 1806 Fossett was joined in her kitchen apprenticeship by her sister-in-law Frances Gillette Hern. The dish remained a favorite at the plantation, so much so that in 1807 Jefferson received a bill for an 80-pound Parmesan cheese80-pound parmesan cheese and 60 pounds of Naples macaroni, which his European agent purchased in Italy. Over the years at Monticello, macaroni and cheese were a standard on the menu. Records show that

Jefferson's last grocery order, placed five months before he died in 1826, included 112 lbs. of macaroni.

History must acknowledge the contributions of enslaved African Americans who took an Italian dish and perfected it to the point that it became one of the most popular dishes in American history. Now you know.

Chapter 28

Integrating the Sky: The First Black Paratrooper of the US Military

Today, being an airborne paratrooper comes with a sense of pride that only someone inside can understand, while those on the outside are left to wonder. While airborne operations are no longer a part of conventional combat deployment, it serves as a time-honored tradition that harkens back to the days of America's participation in the European theater. Black paratroopers can trace their lineage back to one airborne soldier. This is his story.

Walter Morris was born in Waynesboro, GA in 1921. By trade, he was a bricklayer, but by 1942, he was a sSoldier in the US Army stationed at Fort Benning, GA. Morris served as the First Sergeant of his company at the pay grade of E5 because the company didn't have a First Sergeant assigned to them. Company morale was deficient because of racism, segregation, and boredom. His company was responsible for cleaning the airborne obstacle course and guarding the airborne complex overnight after all the white paratroopers completed training for the day.

To improve morale and stay sharp, SGT Morris had his men run the obstacle course while cleaning and getting in formation and exercise. One day Lieutenant General Ridgley Gaither happened to be passing the course and saw these Black men running and exercising. Curious, the General ordered his aid to have SGT Morris report to his office. General Gaither explained to Morris that he had received orders to start a Black airborne test platoon that would become a Black company for the airborne battalion. Walter Morris was made 1SG of this new all-Black unit, the 555th Paratroop Infantry Company, for his leadership. On 8 February 1944, 1SG Morris and 16 others graduated from Airborne School to become the first Black paratroopers.

The 555th Parachute Infantry Battalion earned the moniker "Triple ~~Nickles~~Nickels" due to its number designation, and 17 of the original 20 members of the "colored test platoon" were chosen from the 92nd Infantry (Buffalo) Division. Hence, the phrase "Buffalo ~~Nickles~~Nickels" originated. The trademark is a triangle or pyramid formed by three buffalo nickels connected.

The men of the Triple ~~Nickles~~Nickels were ready and prepared to go to Europe to engage the Nazis, but a shift in the war caused a change in their orders. In late April 1945, the battalion received new orders - a "permanent change of station" to Pendleton Air Base in Pendleton, Oregon, for duty with the U.S. Ninth Service Command on a "highly classified" mission in the U.S. Northwest. The Triple Nickels went to Oregon to fight fires caused by Japanese bombs dropped via balloons. Because of this mission, the 555th became known as "Smoke Jumpers."

In December 1947, General James Gavin, Commander of the 82nd Airborne Division, issued an order incorporating the 555th into the 82nd Airborne. This is significant because the Commander of the 82nd Airborne Division effectively integrated the unit eight months before President Harry Truman signed an executive order legally combining the entire armed forces.

The professionalism, poise, and sheer tenacity of Walter Morris and the 555th Triple Nickels led the charge to break down segregation barriers and force leadership at the highest levels to accept Black paratroopers. Now you know.

Chapter 29

What Could Have Been: America's First HBCU That Didn't Happen

Historically Black Colleges and Universities have a long and vital history within the fabric of African American academics and social life. These institutions have served as the incubators of revolution, progressive thought, and stratification. Like the Black church, the Black college has nurtured its students and infused them with academic knowledge and social experience. No institution outside the Black church can claim to be as influential and productive as the Black college.

Today there are 107 HBCUs; over time, 18 have shut their doors, with ten directly resulting from financial distress. HBCUs are famous for their alums, academic excellence, sports, Greek life, and social atmospheres. Each HBCU is part of a legacy, and each adds to the collective heritage of Black excellence in education.

The distinction of being the first Historically Black College and University goes to Cheyney University. It was founded on 25 February 1837 in Pennsylvania. The University of the District of Columbia was founded in 1851, followed by Lincoln University in 1854 and my home Wilberforce University in 1856. As storied as these HBCUs are, there is little known history regarding what could have been…the HBCU set to predate them all.

Around 1831, Simeon Jocelyn was the driving force behind the endeavors to build a "negro college" in New Haven, Connecticut. Jocelyn made a connection with Arthur Tappan, who supported the concept by acquiring land in the southern portion of New Haven for the institution. He also set aside $1,000 to aid with fundraising. The two men pitched the proposal to the attendees at the Convention of Free People of Color in collaboration with abolitionist William Loyd Garrison. The idea of a neo-colonial university energized the convention and was warmly received. ~~Simeon Jocelyn was the impetus behind the efforts to establish a "Negro college" in New Haven, Connecticut, around 1831. Jocelyn connected with Arthur Tappan, who committed to the idea by purchasing land for the college in the southern part of New Haven. Additionally, he saved $1000 to help with fundraising. The two men joined forces with abolitionist William Loyd Garrison and proposed the idea to the attendees at the Convention of Free People of Color. The~~

~~idea of a negro school for higher education galvanized the convention and was met with much enthusiasm.~~

The location of New Haven was intentionally chosen since it is close to Yale University, a prestigious all-white university. Jocelyn was confident Yale would approve of the new Negro institution and acknowledge it as a college or university for free people of color. On September 7th, 1831, Jocelyn addressed the members of his church about his proposal for a school for Blacks. A town meeting was immediately summoned by Mayor Dennis Kimberly for September 10th to vote on motions rejecting the "negro college." ~~New Haven was chosen specifically for its proximity to Yale University, a prestigious all-white Institution. Jocelyn believed Yale would accept the new Negro school and recognize it as a place of higher education for free people of color. On September 7th, 1831, Jocelyn spoke of his idea for a school for Blacks to the congregation at his home church. Immediately, Mayor Dennis Kimberly called a town meeting for September 10th to vote on resolutions opposing the "Negro College."~~

The New Haven Advertiser published an article the following day proposing the establishment of a new black institution near Cornwall, Connecticut, far from Yale University. Members of Yale University and New Haven's political elite created a committee. Together, they came up with two resolutions claiming that an African American school would "harm Yale College" and other nearby institutions by undermining them and threatening the country's stability. These two resolutions were accepted by a combined vote of 700–4 and stopped any plans to build a "negro college" in New Haven. Simeon Jocelyn was alone in opposition to approximately 600 of his neighbors, who were all critical of the college.

Only James Donaghe and Roger Sherman Baldwin, who would later act as the Amistad hostages, have voted with him. Because of their work establishing a Black college to educate Blacks in the North, neither Baldwin nor Jocelyn are today respected at Yale. No Black people attended Yale College as students before Edward Alexander Bouchet earned his B.A. in the class of 1874, according to Yale historian George Pierson.

~~University and New Haven's political elite created a committee. Together, they came up with two resolutions claiming that an African American school would "harm Yale College" and other nearby institutions by undermining them and threatening the country's stability. These two resolutions were accepted by a combined vote of 700-4 and stopped any plans to build a "Negro college" in New Haven. Simeon Jocelyn was alone in opposition to approximately 600 of his neighbors, who were all critical of the college.~~

~~It is known that only James Donaghe and Roger Sherman Baldwin, who would subsequently represent the Amistad hostages, voted with him. Neither Baldwin nor Jocelyn is recognized now at Yale because of their efforts to build a black college to educate Blacks in the North. Before Edward Alexander Bouchet obtained his B.A. in the class of 1874, according to Yale historian George Pierson, "no blacks attended Yale College as students."~~

After the failure of the New Haven effort, the resiliency of people sympathetic to the education of Blacks persisted until America had its first college dedicated to educating free people of color. Now you know.

History has its eyes on you

Chapter 30

Do You Have the Password: Black Secret Societies and Clandestine Organizations in the Negro Community

Because of Hollywood depictions and gross generalizations, society often associates secret societies with ancient and modern elite whites. Because of geopolitics, classism, government influence, and economic stratification, society also tends to believe that these secret societies fundamentally shape the world in one way or another. Far more surprising is how little the Black community knows about Black secret societies.

Minimal scholarship exists on Negro secret societies. In 1910, author Howard W. Odum included a short chapter called "Fraternal Organizations and Benevolent Societies" in his monograph entitled *Social and Mental Traits of the Negro.* Black secret societies usually fall into two categories, active and ceremonial. Most Negro secret societies in America have been formal, i.e., lodges and fraternal orders. We can interpret from the records that Blacks joined these secret societies for fellowship, mutual aid, protection, belonging, and clandestine planning. Evidence also suggests that at its height, Black secret societies began to compete with the Black church for prominence in nNegro life.

Up until modern times, Freemasonry and Elks lodges were considered secret societies. As perspectives changed, a consorted effort began to dislodge these organizations from the label of a secret society and replace it with the moniker of "a society with secrets." This is because the term "secret society" took on an elitist, corrupt, and influential governmental label that didn't sit well with the modern public.

The first secret society which the negro joined was the Odd Fellows. Its first negro lodge, Philomathean Lodge number 646, emerged in New York in 1843. On August 11th, 1846, a Black secret society was formed to end slavery. Twelve Black men from several states came together to create an organization to recruit members, arm them, and then execute an insurgency. Many members were already members of the Prince Hall Masonic lodges and the AME church. While meeting in St. Louis, they took the name the Twelve Knights of Liberty. They were sworn to secrecy, and part of their oath was the phrase, "I can die, but I cannot reveal the name of any member until the slaves are free." As their numbers swelled to over 1,000 members, they looked to maintain strict secrecy and secretly changed their name to the Order of the Twelve. They also carried a second name, the Knights of Tabor. They even had a female auxiliary known as the Daughters of the Tabernacle.

In 1847, an established secret society opened its ranks to Blacks with the purpose of "restoring the lost Negro to society." The Independent Order of Good Samaritans and its auxiliary group, the Daughters of Samaria, allowed Negro membership on the strict condition that white Samaritans could neither preside over nor meet with Black Samaritans. Black members were only allowed to vote on matters concerning Black people. Eventually, white members left the secret society altogether, and by 1877, there came an end to racially mixed membership in national private organizations.

At the time of the Civil War, there were at least three secret societies among Negroes: Prince Hall Masons, The Odd Fellows, and the Knights of Tabor. 1869 the Ancient Order of Workmen emerged as a ritualistic secret society. The Knights and Daughters of I Will Arise, and the Order of Lone Star Race Pride, Friendship, Love, and Help were other secret societies that emerged. Daughters of Bethlehem, Knights of Canaan, Grand United Order of the Children of Israel, Builders of the Walls of Jerusalem, Household of Ruth, Afro-American Order of Owls.

In 1881, The Grand United Order of True Reformers rose and had arguably the best success. The True Reformers had grown from a hundred members to seventy thousand in twenty- three years. The society had expended more than $2,000,000 in reliefs and benefits and owned $400,000 worth of real estate, a savings bank, a newspaper, a chain of grocery stores, a hotel, and an old folk's home.

In 1902 Booker T. Washington stated that there were about twenty national Negro secret societies. In addition to the True Reformers, he listed the better known as being the Prince Hall Masons, Odd Fellows, Colored Knights of Pythias, United Brothers of Friendship and Sisters of the Mysterious Ten, Elks, Knights of Tabor, Buffaloes, Foresters, Galilean Fishermen, Samaritans, Nazarites, Sons and Daughters of Jacob, Seven Wise Men, Knights of Honor, and the Mosaic Templars of America.

The history of Negro secret societies has vanished from the archives and disappeared from oral history. What few records that do remain reveal to us is that these organizations significantly contributed to the intellect and material building of the Negro race.

What cannot be argued is that no other organization, except the church, could boast of reaching the masses of the negro population like the Black secret society. Now you know.

Chapter 31

Black Smoke: A History of African American BBQ Traditions

Fire, meat, seasoning, and smoke are symbiotic relationships in the Black community. On any given day, for any occasion, Black people will fire up the grill and BBQ. This speaks not only to tradition but also to how intrinsically connected the culture is to the food. BBQ is more than a pastime in the Black community. It is a form of art. It is where traditions meet legacy, and where secrets are passed from generation to generation. It is where relationships are developed and repaired. It is where oral traditions live and where reputations are earned. African Americans and the rule of BBQ is as much the story of Blacks in the New World as slavery is.

In examining the earliest accounts of BBQ in the New World, we are whisked back to 1513 when the Indigenous People of the Caribbean were found to be cooking iguanas, fish, and rabbits over wood fires. These early accounts are from the writings of Christopher Columbus and his crew, who, not surprisingly, stole the food from the Taino people. In South Carolina, on the island of Saint Helena, there are Spanish accounts of the indigenous peoples slowly cooking whole hog in the 1560s.

To understand Black BBQ, credence must be given to the Native American foundation of barbecue. Although history is shallow on the subject, historical accounts remind us of the Taino in the Caribbean cooking in this manner and early indigenous peoples across America, especially in and around Virginia. Indigenous cuisine involved smoking meats such as bison, elk, and rabbit. It also involved the use of spices and chilies. Therefore, Black sSmoke as we know it today is a mixture of Indigenous, West African, and European meat-smoking techniques.

What we are sure of is that this barbecuing animal over fire transmogrified from a survival tactic to an art form with the amalgamation of enslaved Blacks. Historical writings and oral history clearly illustrate how bonded people infused traditional African practices of "seasoning" meats into their methodology. The use of herbs and spices greatly enhanced flavor. They also added the technique of slow roasting, off-set cooking, searing, and underground cooking into their repertoire. -Culinary historian Andrian Miller says, "We have newspaper articles in the 1800s saying, to have an authentic barbecue, you must have a negro man or colored man-... so it's almost like African

Americans are part of the recipe. You couldn't have a good barbecue without African Americans involved. So that's how prominent African Americans were."

Pitmasters were senior enslaved people who were great cooks and spearheaded the effort to prepare the BBQ for the slaveholders. Younger enslaved persons learned how to prepare a whole hog for a BBQ from the pitmaster. Pitmaster was coined during the dark days of servitude when these elderly cooks cooked in earthen pits. The Daily Times-News of Burlington, North Carolina, reported the first recorded printed reference to a pitmaster on September 22, 1939. ~~The term *pitmaster* refers to an elderly slave who was an expert cook and led the effort to prepare the BBQ for the slaveholders. Younger enslaved people worked under the *pitmaster* to learn how to prepare a whole hog for a BBQ." The term *pitmaster* was born in the dark times of enslavement when these elderly cooks barbecued using earthen pits. The earliest known printed reference to a pitmaster was published on September 22, 1939, by the *Daily Times-News* of Burlington, North Carolina.~~

The subterranean pit was the most prevalent strategy employed by bond people during the Civil War and freemen afterward. Learning to smoke meat in an early pit is a proper art form practiced far into the twentieth century. According to pitmaster and whole hog expert Dr. Howard Conyers, this "hole in the ground" approach was frequently used in the Black community until the 1970s. This method differs from that employed by Indigenous peoples who smoked above ground. ~~The underground pit was the most popular technique used by bond people in the antebellum and freemen post-Civil War. Learning to smoke meat in an early pit is a proper art form and was used well into the 20th century. According to Dr. Howard Conyers, pitmaster and whole hog expert, this "hole in the ground" technique was widely employed in the black community until the 1970s. This is a shift from the method used by Indigenous peoples who smoked above ground.~~

Unfortunately, the names of many barbecue pioneers have been lost to history. By the time of the Civil War, Southerners had been cooking barbecue for more than two centuries, and many of these cooks were enslaved African Americans. After the Civil War, thousands of talented cooks in rural areas and small towns delighted generations of hungry Southerners. Still, their names disappeared into newspapers and other historical records.

Pitmaster Marie Jean oversaw a BBQ. She was a Black woman who 1840, led a group of men in preparing a noteworthy Fourth of July supper. The fact that she was a Black woman who was enslaved and living in Arkansas two decades before the Civil War, who was recognized for her cooking skills in the local paper, and who was finally able to buy her freedom and own a restaurant is astonishing.

The wonderful sauce made by "Old" Arthur Watts, born into slavery in Randolph County, Missouri 1837, is still bottled and sold by his heirs. Arthur was introduced to open pit grilling at six as an oppressed child. While in service in his teens, he began making innovative foods. He laboriously perfected these recipes while living freely till his death at 108. ~~The delectable sauce that "Old" Arthur Watts, born into slavery in Randolph County, Missouri 1837, produced is still bottled and offered for sale by his descendants. Around six, Arthur was introduced to open pit grilling as an enslaved person. He started creating original dishes in his teens while being held in servitude. He laboriously improved these recipes while living in freedom until his passing at 108.~~

Mrs. M.E. Abrams told Caldwell Sims in Union in late February 1937 about a weekend custom among slave relatives: roasting a hog to grill. Her BBQ story can be found in the seventeen-volume book *Slave Narratives: A Folk History of Slavery in the United States* from "Interviews with Former Enslaved People."

Mr. Wesley Jones described his early BBQ experience in his slave memoirs. "I used to stay up all night the night before dem barbecues, making and basting the meats with barbecue sauce. It's made with vinegar, salt, butter, black and red pepper, basil, onion, garlic, and a little sage. Some folks put sugar in it." This story repeats a few themes: barbecue is for special occasions, barbecue is for political purposes, barbecue is a reason to celebrate and enjoy oneself, and enslaved people create barbecue. What's noteworthy is that Mr. B includes a recipe for vinegar-based barbecue sauce and a firsthand explanation of barbecue.

~~meats with barbecue sauce the night before dem barbecues. It contains vinegar, salt, butter, black and red pepper, basil, onion, garlic, and a small amount of sage. Some people add some sugar to it. A few themes are repeated in this story: barbecue is for special events, barbeque is for political reasons, barbecue is a reason to celebrate and enjoy, and enslaved people prepare barbecue. What's intriguing is that Mr. B gives us a recipe for vinegar-based barbecue sauce and a first-hand account of how barbecue was prepared.~~

<u>Abby Fisher was born in South Carolina in 1832. She was raised as an enslaved person and was taught as a cook in plantation kitchens. Fisher briefly lived in Alabama after recovering her freedom before returning to San Francisco. She gave the recipes to others, who assisted her in publishing What Mrs. Fisher Knew About Old Southern Cooking in 1881. Mrs. Fisher was illiterate and incapable of writing. Fisher's monograph includes the recipe for "Game Sauce," which is the best in the world and goes exceptionally well with barbeque.</u> ~~In South Carolina in 1832, Abby Fisher was born. She was reared as an enslaved person and trained as a cook while working in plantation kitchens. After regaining her freedom, Fisher briefly resided in Alabama before~~

~~relocating to San Francisco. She transcribed the recipes to others, who helped her publish the book *What Mrs. Fisher Knew About Old Southern Cooking in 1881*. Mrs. Fisher was illiterate and could not write. The recipe for "Game Sauce," which is regarded as the best in the world and is considered to go incredibly well with barbeque, is provided by Fisher in the monograph.~~

Unfortunately, the tradition of barbecue cooking is saturated with racism, just like every other institution of American life. The contributions of the Indigenous peoples have been all but erased from the history of barbecue. Until recently, there was significant progress in erasing the legacy of African Americans from barbecue history. Until 2019, the American Royal Barbecue Hall of Fame inducted 27 pit masters into its ranks, and only one was Black.

Whether they publicly acknowledge it or not, the history of barbecue is only possible with the contributions of African Americans. Now you know.

Chapter 32

Discovering King Tut's Tomb, Give Credit Where Credit Is Due

Perhaps the most significant archaeological find in Egypt was the discovery of the tomb of Pharaoh Tutankhamun. Uncovered in 1922, the find proved to be the most valuable treasure discovery because it was so hidden, grave robbers were unable to discover and loot it. All the treasures of King Tut were perfectly preserved, along with his body and anything he would need in the afterlife. King Tut lay in peace for 3,000 years.

History has credited the discovery of King Tut's tomb to British archaeologist Howard Carter. Some websites and historians give Howard full credit, excluding the Egyptians who discovered the tomb. Other historians and organizations will attribute the discovery to Howard Carter "and his team." What is consistent about the narrative is that it remains whitewashed and seeks to hide the name of the person who discovered the tomb. His name ~~character~~ must be said because his historical place cannot be erased. Here is an accurate account of how King Tutankhamun's tomb was discovered.

Howard Carter had been searching for tombs for six unsuccessful years. The excavation was almost canceled because of lacking evidence that a grave would be found. But Carter convinced his financer, Lord Carnarvon, to give him another season to search. He fully believed he could discover a tomb in this section of the Valley of Kings.

The initial stone step, which led down to the tomb, was discovered by accident on November 4th, 1922, by a young water boy named Hussein Abdel Rasoul. Twice a day, he would bring large pottery jars filled with water to the excavation site for the workers. The pots were tied with rope and placed on the back of a donkey to make the journey. The boy would take the jars off the donkey and set them in the sand at the site. However, because the jars were rounded on the bottom, he would have to dig out some sand to set the pots in so they would remain upright. While swishing the sand away that miraculous day, he uncovered a flat stone that looked as if it was sculpted. He began wiping away sand until he found a large surface. This surface was the first step down into the boy pharaoh's tomb. Rasoul rushed to tell the workers of his find, which is how King Tut's tomb was discovered.

A photograph captures the boy's exceptional part in the discovery. After the tomb was excavated, Howard Carter placed a necklace from the grave over his head, acknowledging that this tomb may not have ever been discovered had it not been for the young boy and his jars of water. The Sacred Scarab necklace was only one of the many treasures found below the sands he had first scraped away. This treasure now hung on his neck as a result. Years later, the young boy, now an older man, held the photograph of himself enjoying that moment. Later, the son of that once young boy had the photo with the older man holding the picture.

Unfortunately, Western history hasn't dared to credit young Hussein Abdel Rasoul for his discovery. Instead, history admonished Howard Carter and bestowed all recognition upon him. Yet, in Egypt, it is prevalent to hear tour guides and locals tell the authentic story of the discovery, restoring Hussein to his rightful place in history. Now you know.

Chapter 33

Climbing to God: The All-Black Group That Scaled Mt. Everest

Towering 29,031 ft into the heavens, Mt Everest is one of the most spectacular natural formations on the face of the earth and the highest. In the small mountain climbing community, Everest is the most recognizable name. About 4,000 people have successfully reached the summit, and yet, until recently, only eight of them have been Black. That has recently changed.

The Full Circle climbing group came together to change the narrative for the Black community, particularly in the United States, and how we interact with outdoor spaces. But to understand the significance of their accomplishment, you must understand the legacy which they stand on.

Sophia Danenberg was the first African American and Black woman to climb Mount Everest. What makes her assent so remarkable is that Danenberg only decided to climb Everest one week before starting her journey. She was initially slated to summit Cho Oyu, the sixth tallest mountain in the world.

Sophia Danenberg began climbing Mount Everest unguided, choosing her route, carrying her gear, and making her own decisions at age 34. At 7 A.M. on May 19, 2006, Danenberg reached the top of Mount Everest. Withstanding bad weather during the night that delayed some other climbers in her party, two Sherpas were the only climbers to witness the event. At the time, Danenberg was suffering from bronchitis, a stuffed nose, frostbite on her cheeks, and a clogged oxygen mask. Sophia Danenberg was the first African American and Bblack woman to reach the summit.

Following a legacy of perseverance, trailblazing, and defying the odds, the Full Circle climbing group reached Mount Everest's summit on May 12, 2022. As the first all-Black group to accomplish such a feat, they have solidified themselves into the cement of history and challenged prevailing notions regarding Blacks, cold weather, outdoor activities, and extreme sports.

Phil Henderson was the only team member leading the group with previous experience on Mount Everest. The members who reached the summit were Manoah Ainuu, Frederick Campbell, Eddie Taylor, James Kagambi, Desmond Mullins, Thomas Moore, Abby Dione,

Rosemary Saal, and eight Sherpa guides. Henderson did not attempt the summit on this trip.

This team of climbers came together with the mission of climbing the highest mountain in the world, and in doing so, they climbed over all the racist troupes, scaled past ideas of inferiority, and successfully climbed to God. Now you know.

Chapter 34

The Wereth Eleven: The Forgotten Black Soldiers of WWII

One of the great tragedies of the US Armed Forces is their historical approach to race relations. In this area, the Armed Forces ~~have a pathetic~~ need a better track record of acknowledging and memorializing the efforts and sacrifices of Afr~~o~~ican-American contributions to the war effort. The military prides itself on tradition and telling its own story. They've erected museums and memorials to support this endeavor. Yet, the Armed Forces ~~fall miserably short in highlighting and spreading authentic information surrounding i~~must highlight and spread authentic information ab~~ts A~~out Afr~~o~~ican-American contributions. This is an effort to tell the stories of those ~~Afro-Americans~~ Black people whom the US Armed Forces chose to forget systematically.

The 333rd Field Artillery Battalion was a segregated African American unit deployed to Europe to participate in the Battle of the Bulge. The 333rd was equipped with the M1-155mm howitzer and ~~had a high reputation as being~~ was highly regarded as incredibly accurate on the battlefield. Their precision was renowned, and units would call in the assistance of the 333rd regularly. The German onslaught was so massive and overwhelming that the commander of the 106th Artillery Division ordered a retreat...that excluded batteries of the 333rd, who were called to stay back and provide cover while the others pulled back. The Germans captured Schönberg and, continuing to advance, shattered much of the 333rd Field Artillery Battalion, killing or capturing half of its men.

Eleven Black men were captured but later managed to escape while being forced to march back to German lines. After walking for six ~~6~~ hours in the freezing snow with only two rifles among them, they stumbled into a town. They were generously taken in by Mathias and Maria Langer, who were Allied supporters.

A neighbor who was sympathetic to the Germans betrayed them. Shortly after, a German patrol arrived at the house they were taking refuge in. The Americans had the misfortune to fall into the hands of troops of the 1st SS, Adolf Hitler's deadly Panzer Division. The SS had a dark history of extreme torture, brutality, and inhuman acts. They were often jacked up on meth and quenched their thirst for death in the blood of others.

These eleven African American men were marched into the woods and tortured. Their fingers were sliced off, and their eyes were poked out. They all had stab wounds on their bodies. Apart from being shot, the skulls of the soldiers had been smashed by what appeared to be rifle butts. They also had broken legs. All were shot repeatedly in a way meant to cause excruciating pain but not kill. They were mutilated and left for dead in early December.

It was in the early days of February 1945 that anyone would know what fate had befallen the eleven soldiers. As winter came to an end, the snow began to recede. Mathias and his family were on their way to church when they saw frozen hands sticking out of the snow. The eleven men were discovered in February when the snow began to thaw.

However, nobody paid attention to the eleven guys who died at Wereth. The same US Army investigators who unearthed the horror of the Malmedy Massacre also uncovered all the information about what transpired at Wereth, including that the Back men who died there had been mercilessly tortured, unlike the white dead at Malmedy. However, even though many local citizens, including those protected by the artillerymen, were still alive and could have offered evidence, the investigators did not investigate the case further and took no testimony.

A subcommittee of the Senate Committee on Armed Services examined in detail the atrocities committed by the Nazis during the Battle of the Bulge in 1949, but it completely disregarded the Wereth tragedy. In letters, the troops' families in the U.S. were informed that their loved ones had died in combat.

Remember the men of the Wereth 11: Curtis Adams of South Carolina, Mager Bradley of Mississippi, George Davis, Jr., of Alabama, Thomas Forte of Mississippi, Robert Green of Georgia, James Leatherwood of Mississippi, Nathaniel Moss of Texas, George Motten of Texas, William Pritchett of Alabama, James Stewart of West Virginia, and Due Turner of Arkansas. Now you know.

Chapter 35

Black Women and Violence: A Gendered Analysis of Armed Resistance

In the discourse of self-defense and Black liberation, the Black man is often highlighted for his strategic use of the gun to repeal racial violence and assert himself as a man and citizen. While the Black woman is regulated to the shadows, rarely mentioned but as an accomplice to a man, like a less-popular sidekick. This could be furthest from the truth.

Some believe Black women have only used Bibles, pens, and bodies to defend themselves and their community. Black women turned to armed resistance early and often. As non-violent tactics were met with violent acts from white violent actors, Black women revised their strategy. They picked up the gun (and other weapons) to save themselves, their family, and their extended people. In doing so, Black women challenged the prevailing notions of violence and masculinity. The gun is most associated with man and citizenship. Black women used it in an assertion of their rights and their place on the social hierarchy.

When Black women and armed resistance enter the discourse, it is usually to espouse known revolutionaries such as Harriet Tubman, Stagecoach Mary, Ida B. Wells, women of the Black Panther Party, and Cathay Williams, the only Black female member of the Buffalo Soldiers. Yet, there are so many more.

For instance, author Jasmin Young in her dissertation entitled *Strapped*, asserts that during the Reconstruction era, Black women served as armed guards while men voted. In 1865, a Black woman in South Carolina, known only as Rose, led an armed slave rebellion of 27 outlaws. She was promptly executed upon capture and erased from the history books.

Mabel Williams, the wife of Robert F. Williams, who founded the Monroe, NC Chapter of the NAACP, was a stark supporter of armed resistance. She formed the gun club, the Union City Rifle Club, in 1957. She used the gun to repel the North Carolina Ku Klux Klan, who attempted to murder her and her family. Mabel was often at odds with the civil rights movement because of her advocacy of violence to resist racial terror. Unfortunately, history only chose to remember the armed resistance of Robert F. Williams, a consequence of the gendered ideology of the day.

Ms. Asa Lee was a Black woman in NC who publicly and violently faced the Ku Klux Klan and the chief of police over the rights of Blacks to use a public pool. Gloria Richardson was another Black woman who advocated using armed resistance for self-defense against anti-Black violence. She was the leader of the Cambridge Movement, and her vocal promotion of the use of guns changed the organization's direction. The Cambridge Movement underwent a paradigm shift from being anti-violent to employing armed self-defense and retaliatory violence, all under the leadership of a Black woman.

In Greenwood, Mississippi, Laura McGhee opened her home to SNCC volunteers in town to organize a voting drive. She guarded her home and guest by sitting on her porch at night with her rifle. On 3 April 1964, McGhee fought an officer in a bare-knuckle fight who pushed her during a demonstration. In another incident, McGhee went to the police station to retrieve her son, who was arrested. The Chief of Police refused to let her into a room with her lawyer and son and pushed her back. McGhee punched him in his eye so hard that he fell unconscious.

A lady in Mississippi named Mrs. Spinks sat up all night with her shotgun, waiting on the KKK while her out-of-town guest slept under her protection. In 1965, a Black woman named Fay Bellamy was engaged in hand-to-hand combat with a Georgia State Trooper on the steps of the Georgia Capital. After being arrested for protesting, a jailer attempted to assault her, and she hit him as hard as she could across his face and knocked him off his feet.

Daisy Bates, advisor to the Little Rock Nine, knew the effectiveness of armed resistance. Her home was heavily armed, and she fired her gun several times at those who sought to harm her. Rebecca Wilson of Dallas, Georgia, defied terrorists with pistol fire. Seven hooded men showed up at her door, and she fired five shots, killing one man and wounding another. In Carroll County, Mississippi, Leola Blackmon used firearms against night riders who attempted to stifle voter registration.

These are a few examples of Black women employing armed resistance to meet the force of racial violence with the strength of Black woman power. History has minimal scholarship on Black women engaged in violence due to the presence of misogyny and the idea that protecting the Black family was the job of the Black man. Let the record show that despite the almost non-existent discourse, Black women were there from the beginning, offering themselves up in any way necessary to combat anti-Black violence. Now you know.

150   History has its eyes on you

Chapter 36

The Case of Willie Francis, the Black Teen Who Got the Electric Chair Twice

Willie Francis was a young, Black man in Louisiana who is best known for surviving an attempt to execute him by electric chair. Here's his story. In 1944, Willie Francis was arrested for the murder of Andrew Thomas, a pharmacist Willie had worked for more than nine months prior. Thomas had been shot and killed, but the killer was unknown. Willie was detained in Texas for being in the wrong place at the wrong time. Police claimed he was carrying Thomas' wallet in his pocket, though no evidence of this claim was submitted during the trial.

When Willie Francis first claimed that other people were involved in the murder, the authorities rejected his assertions. Shortly after, while being questioned, Francis admitted to killing Thomas and stated, "It was a secret about me and him." In his 2008 book, *The Execution of Willie Francis,* author Gilbert King references tales in St. Martinville about the pharmacist sexually abusing young people. Willie was questioned while still a kid and without the presence of a guardian or attorney, which is against the law according to the sixth amendment.

Later, Francis gave the police instructions on where to look for the holster that contained the murder weapon. Near the crime scene, a gun used to kill Thomas was discovered. It belonged to a St. Martinville deputy sheriff who had previously threatened to kill Thomas. Just before the trial, the gun and the bullets found at the crime site and on Thomas' body vanished from police evidence.

The court-appointed defense attorneys made no objections, brought no witnesses, and presented no defense during his trial. Even though Francis was without legal representation at the time of the claimed confession, the reason did not contest the veracity of his statements. Despite being underage, aged 15 at the time of the incident, Francis was easily found guilty of murder two days after the trial started and was given the death penalty by the judge and twelve jurors.

Francis avoided being put to death via the electric chair on May 3, 1946. Witnesses said the teenager screamed in pain from under the leather hood. It was discovered that "Gruesome Gertie," a portable electric chair, had been incorrectly set up by a drunken prison officer and convict from the Louisiana State Penitentiary at Angola. The jail officials chose to abort the execution after going through the agony of a botched execution.

Bertrand DeBlanc, a young attorney, decided to take Francis' case. He believed that being put to death once more was an unfair, harsh, and unusual punishment against the Constitution. *Francis v. Resweber* was DeBlanc's appeal to the Supreme Court, and he argued that there had been several Fifth, Eighth, and Fourteenth Amendment rights violations. These included infractions of double jeopardy, harsh and unusual punishment, and equal protection.

The US Supreme Court dismissed the appeal in yet another ridiculous ruling from the highest court in the land. For his final dinner, Willie ordered his favorite dish: fried chicken. It was Friday, and Willie, a devout Catholic, chose not to consume the chicken. On May 9, 1947, Willie Francis was executed again in the electric chair. He passed away young, helpless, and hungry. At age 16, he was placed in the electric chair for the first time, and at age 18, he was executed. Now you know.

Chapter 37

The History of the Highway System

The idea and strategic planning for a highway system had its genesis in 1916. Yet, the project is named after President Dwight D Eisenhower. Eisenhower championed the Federal Aid Highway Act in 1956, which granted funding to the highway system project. But he was not president in 1916 when the idea first came about. Eisenhower was an officer stationed in Germany and saw the effectiveness of having a highway system, but he still needed to come up with the idea. The idea was born in 1916 after a series of events that showed the US Government that it needed an effective way to move troops and supplies in the event of. The question is, what were those events?

WWI started in 1914. Congress sold the idea of a highway system to the people using a fear tactic. They told the people that America needed a highway system to quickly move troops and supplies in the event of an invasion. The only problem was that there was no threat of attack from a foreign government. The enemy was Germans, Austrians, Ottomans, and Bulgaria, none of which could invade the United States. So, the idea of a highway system was sold to the public out of fear. Many in the Black community subscribe to the belief that the more sinister reason the government decided they needed a highway system was a series of events before that, which compelled the government to make provisions for what could happen next.

Looking back, we can see that America had a serious problem with racial riots and unrest. Racial conflicts were an explosive part of American culture, from the riots in Atlanta in 1906 to Illinois, Texas, and beyond. Due to extremely high racial tensions (slavery ended less than 50 years prior), rebellions often flared at a moment's notice, often from police brutality, inequality, and injustice. ~~(Ironically, the same issues we are rebelling against today).~~

These riots showed that the US Government was not prepared logistically to move in federal troops if needed due to the lack of a highway system. After the government studied this observation, they concluded that a highway system was the best practice to open the logistical lines to move "troops and supplies" across the United States. The highway system was disguised as a deterrent against foreign incursion while it was a control method.

The government called on General Blackjack Pershing to draw a map that he deemed (from the US Army's perspective) the best routes that connected urban developments, military facilities, and any other COGs (centers of gravity). This map covered 20,000 miles and became known as Pershing's Map. The government adopted Pershing's map, and President Dwight D Eisenhower championed the highway system's construction, the genesis of what we now know as the Dwight D Eisenhower Transportation System. Now you know.

Chapter 38

Identifying Unknown Graves of the Enslaved

Racism is s such a powerful virus that it extends from one life into the next, from the living to the dead. Historians and anthropologists continually search for the unmarked graves of former bond people, and in doing so, some very distinct patterns have emerged. The following context will help anyone to identify the final resting place of the sons and daughters of Africa who rest on the earth without identification.

It's important to understand that the luxury of headstones was often denied to the Negro. Additionally, de sure segregation said the Negro could not be buried with whites, thereby regulating Blacks to a grave separated from others. These separated graves were known as a Potters Field.

Yucca Plants have been used to mark the graves of the enslaved going back several hundred years. One reason they were used is because of their resiliency. The Yucca houseplant lives for about five years, but a yucca tree lives for several decades. Some varieties of yucca take 50 years to reach their mature size. From a spiritual and cultural perspective, yucca plants were used because they symbolize motherhood, eternity, and mourning and are said to ward off evil spirits. Yucca Plants are also said to keep restless spirits in their graves.

Another way to mark the graves of the enslaved was to use shells. The practice has been traced back to the BaKongo belief that seashells enclose the soul's immortal presence. The Gullah people of the sea islands off the coast of South Carolina and Georgia often used the method.

The periwinkle plant is believed to be the most widely used wildflower at the graves of enslaved Americans. It is a ground-covering plant that produces lavender-blue colors in its flowers. It has a propensity to smother weeds, and therefore, bond people often use it to mark the graves of the dead. Additionally, the smell of crushed foliage is a deterrent to dogs and some animals, which prevents them from digging in that area. Lastly, the plant thrives in soil whose pH is altered by decaying bodies and thus is unbothered by highly acidic or bare ground.

Another technique was to engrave secret symbols into whatever was near, such as a headstone (if available), a rock, or a tree. If a grave did have a monument, very few were inscribed with the typical epitaphs we are accustomed to. Many had symbols, backward written letters, initials, and scrambled words. According to Dr. Lynn Rainville, this intentional secrecy was not born out of a lack of language but, rather, a cultural adaptation to the institution of slavery.

Sometimes children's graves have been marked with pink quartz, a secret message indicating the final resting place of a child. Another technique was to stack stones in a pile. Although these geological formations rarely survive molestation by human hands, evidence of this type of marking has been recorded in the oral history of the formerly enslaved.

The "link system" was found to be explicitly used in Memory Hill Cemetery in Milledgeville, Georgia. The living chose to honor the dead by creating a system of link markers with a particular meaning. One link represented a person who was born into slavery but died free. Two links represent a person born free but later enslaved and died without gaining their freedom. Three links represent those born into slavery, lived as enslaved people and died enslaved. Now you know.

Chapter 39

Black Pirates: Men of African Descent on the High Seas

Piracy is often represented in Hollywood and pop culture as an occupation for European men who sought to navigate, plunder, and raise hell on the world's oceans. Yet, minimal scholarship is given to men of African heritage who were also some of the greatest pirates ever to sail the seas.

The story of Black pirates is, in many ways, the story of slavery. Black mariners were motivated by various factors, such as escaping bondage, runaways, adventurists, or working off debt. Ironically, some Africans served as employees on slave ships and had a slightly higher socio-status than the enslaved Africans in the cargo hold, according to historian Taylor Yangas and the article "Black Pirates in the Golden Age of Piracy."

Slave ships were often attacked and raided by pirates. The African captives were either sold off for financial gain or allowed to be crew members aboard the boat. Prisoners found that life on a pirate ship was extremely labor intensive and one of the most democratic societies of the old world. Every pirate on board the vessel had a say, regardless of ethnicity. Pirates valued skilled labor over race.

Captain Sam Bellemy's crew at one point consisted of more than 50% of formerly enslaved Africans. Some historians assert that Black Beard was the offspring of an English Nobleman and a mulatto servant. What is fact is that at some point, about 30% of Blackbeard's crew was of African heritage.

Black Caesar was a member of the Black Beards crew who served aboard the *Queen Anne's Revenge*. Caesar and Black Beard operated heavily around the Florida Keys circa the early 1700s. Caesar became a crew member after being captive on a slave ship. He and others overtook the captain and escaped the ship. Caesar served with Black Beard until the demise of the famous pirate. Caesar's Rock in Key Largo and a channel named Caesar's Creek are named after him.

Other Black pirates were Henrick Quintor, who served with Sam Bellemy. Diego Grillo was a Black pirate born in Havana with a primarily white-male crew. A pirate ship named *The Good Fortune* was captured by a Black pirate named Old South. Juan Andres was a Black Pirate who plundered along the coast of Venezuela. Peter Cloise was a formerly enslaved person rescued by Edward Davis in 1679.

Black pirates were not subjugated to the racist laws found on land. Black pirates could bear arms, take booty, and vote in a democratic society. Stede Bonnet, a white planter turned pirate, said, "Piracy itself was its race, and it trumped color, nationality, or station of birth. A man called himself a pirate could never be called an enslaved person." Now you know.

Chapter 40

Pablo Picasso: Plagiarism and Denial

History records that in 1920, Pablo Picasso said of African art, "L'art nègre? Connais pas." It meant, "African art? Never heard of it!" It was a bold denial of African influence and the very existence of African art. He implicitly denied that Africans could create works worthy of "art." This was very ironic, if not mischievous, for a man later found with a collection of African art. Had Picasso admitted Africa influenced him, it would have been enough to call him a great artist and end it. Instead, his petty denial of the apparent earned him another title: culture vulture.

Picasso was reportedly blown away by the "magic" of African art. Picasso was introduced to an African sculpture by Henri Matisse, and soon after, Picasso would have a life-changing experience in the Trocadéro's Ethnographic Museum in Paris. His art changed as he looked at the museum's African and Oceanic collections. "And then I understood what painting meant," he later stated of the event. "It's not an artistic process; it's a type of sorcery that stands between us and the hostile universe, a means of grabbing power by imbuing our terrors and desires with form. That day, I realized I'd found my calling." He discovered his calling in Africa. ~~Picasso is said to have been blown away by the "magic" of African art. Henri Matisse exposed Picasso to an African sculpture he had just purchased, and soon after, Picasso was to have a life-changing experience at the Ethnographic Museum of the Trocadéro in Paris. As he looked at the African and Oceanic collection at the museum, his art was taking a shift. He later said of the experience, "And then I understood what painting meant. It's not an aesthetic process; it's a form of magic that interposes itself between us and the hostile universe, a means of seizing power by imposing a form on our terrors and desires. That day I understood that I had found my path." He found his path in African and Oceanic works and denied their influence!~~

"Les Demoiselles d'Avignon," one of Picasso's most famous paintings, conveys the narrative all too well. Here was a man who admired African beauty but couldn't recognize it publicly. Perhaps he was a victim of circumstance, bound so tightly by the chains of white supremacy that any acknowledgment of respect for Africa would have compromised his race. Perhaps he was simply a coward, too afraid to declare to his contemporaries that Africa had stirred his brain and spirit.

It will never be obvious why he decided to be seen as a genius when the source of his genius was dismissed as a savage's habitat. ~~One of Picasso's most famous paintings, the "Les Demoiselles d'Avignon," tells the story all too well. Here was a man enamored with African beauty but, for some reason, could not begin to accept it publicly. Maybe he was a victim of circumstance, tied down by the chains of white supremacy so tight that any admission of appreciation for Africa would have betrayed his race. Maybe he was just a coward too scared to admit to his contemporaries that Africa had moved his intellect and spirit. It will never be clear why he chose to be deemed a genius when the source of that ingenuity was derided as the home of the savages.~~

The African influence in his work emerged as a contentious subject in South Africa in 2006. Picasso's painting was presented alongside 29 African results from Picasso's collection at the Picasso and Africa exhibition. It's an "innovative dialogue between Picasso's work and his African inspiration." However, Sandile Memela, the then-head of the South African Department of Arts and Culture, ~~The African influence inherent in his work resurfaced as a hot issue in 2006 in South Africa. At the Picasso and Africa exhibition, the artist's work was~~

~~displayed together with 29 African results like those in Picasso's collection. It was described as an "innovative dialogue between Picasso's work and his African inspiration." However, Sandile Memela, then the South African Department of Arts and Culture head of communications, would have none. Memela~~ said, "Today, the truth is on display that Picasso would not have been the renowned creative genius he was if he did not steal and re-adapt the work of 'anonymous [African] artists.'" It was a brazen truth that shook tables. But Memela still needed to be finished. He added, "There seems to be some clandestine agenda… that projects Picasso as someone… who loved African art so much that he went out of his way to reveal it to the world… But all this is a whitewash… he is but one of the many products of African inspiration and creativity who lacked the courage to admit its influence on his consciousness and creativity." Now you know.

History has its eyes on you

History has its eyes on you